BLOOMING VIOLET

Two-Act Play (based on a true story)

Written by: JS Jacklin

Dedicated to Rose Maureen

© BLOOMING VIOLET

2023 JS JACKLIN

ISBN: 978-1-7386397-1-7

All rights reserved. No part of this publication may be reproduced, distributed, or transmitted in any form or by any means, including photocopying, recording, or other electronic or mechanical methods, without the prior written permission of the publisher, except in the case of brief quotations embodied in critical reviews and certain other noncommercial uses permitted by copyright law. For permission requests, contact Dot The T Productions at **dotthet@yahoo.com**

Blooming Violet is based on actual events that occurred during the early life of Violet Macdonald. Some creative license has been applied to dramatize incidental gaps with respect to the story line. Most names have been changed to protect identities of certain characters in the story.

For professional performance rights, contact dotthet@yahoo.com.
For digital copies or performance rights in amateur theatre, contact https://playwrightsguild.ca.
To read more about the authors and their other scripts & books; https://jsjacklin.com/

2023 First Edition

Photo credit for Back Cover Photo: *Dylan Bright, 2022*

Photo credit for Front Cover Photo: *Kenneth Croft, 1950*

Permission obtained from family for use of photograph images on the back page

© It's *A Long, Long Way to Tipperary* (Jack Judge & Harry H. Williams)

© *Don't Sit Under the Apple Tree* (Lew Brown & Charles Tobias)

© *We'll Meet Again* (Ross Parker & Hughie Charles)

We extend our gratitude and appreciation to *Rita Dean, Margaret Longmuir, Jackie Godfrey, Tom Oyston* and *Trevor Croft* for clarifying facts and sharing their fond memories of Violet Macdonald's early life. Also helpful were archived pages found on the world-wide-web of the life and times in Stockton-on-Tees and Thornaby-on-Tees during WW1 and WW2. The final version of this script came together following the reading performance from three very talented Yorkshire-born actors. Not only did their rendition lift the characters off the page, but brought the whole story to life, as we had hoped. Thank you to *Jodie Auckland, Emilie Stroud* and *Andy Bartle*.

Blooming Violet

Characters:

11 Characters can be played individually or by 4 actors with multiple roles. The script has been written to accommodate doubling.

FEMALE (1):   **Agnes Wimpole** – *Violet's mother* (15-49 years of age)
                  Lettie – *Violet's best friend* (20-28 years of age)
                  Voice of Mrs. Ashton – (mid-50's)

MALE (1):   **Ernie Ogden** – *Violet's step-father* (16-50 years of age)
                  Ken Lester – *Ken Clarke's best mate* (22-25 years of age)
                  Purser /Vicar – (Non-speaking)

MALE (2):   **Rodney Macdonald** – *Violet's birth father* (21-25 years of age)
                  Ken Clarke – *Violet's husband* (22-26 years of age)
                  Voice of Mr. Ashton – (mid-50's)

FEMALE (2):   **Violet Macdonald** – (8-29 years of age)

Setting:

The action spans the years 1916 to 1952 in England, and follows the life and times of a young VIOLET MACDONALD who passed away at 86 years old on March 2, 2010.

The settings are minimalistic but purposeful in their representations of various locations, including: pubs, front rooms of row houses, bedroom, cow shed, army mess hall, exterior of a factory, ocean liner's interior and deck, posh dining room, the seaside and the New York City port terminal.

Each scene should transition into the next, with little disruption – thus the importance of keeping set pieces to a minimum. Costumes and hair should be detailed to distinguish the changing times. Use of sound and lighting will optimize scene setting. Costume changes are most effective if transitioned on stage, to keep an uninterrupted flow.

The timelines & locations should be shared with the audience throughout – either by projection onto a rear screen or as simple as an easel with large placards that change with each transition.

Most events and relationships are accurate and are representative of not so much an extraordinary life, but of an ordinary, working-class, Yorkshire-woman experiencing extraordinary times.

Scenes:

ACT ONE

1.	September, 1916	The Green Farm, Thornaby-on-Tees, England
2.	October, 1920	Hammersmith Palais Dance Hall, London
3.	1921	London/India
4.	1922	London/India
5.	February, 1923	London/India
6.	April, 1923	London/India
7.	June, 1923	London/India
8.	October, 1923	Thornaby/India
9.	Early December, 1923	Military Hospital, London
10.	March, 1924	Agnes's Family Home, Thornaby
11.	May, 1932	Violet's Family Home, Thornaby
12.	September, 1939	The Ashton's/Violet's Family Home, Thornaby
13.	August, 1940	Violet's Family Home, Thornaby
14.	September, 1943	Head Wrightson & Co, Thornaby
15.	May 8, 1945	The Harewood Arms, Thornaby

ACT TWO

1.	November, 1949	Sergeant's Mess, Stockton-on-Tees, England
2.	July, 1950	Redcar Pier, Northeast Coast, England
3.	February, 1951	St. Paul's Church, Stockton
4.	June, 1951	Ken Clarke's Family Home, Stockton
5.	December, 1951	The Turk's Head, Stockton
6.	March – December, 1952	Canada/England
7.	December 25, 1952	New York City Pier Terminal, U.S.A.

SEPTEMBER 1916

THE GREEN FARM IN THORNABY-ON-TEES, YORKSHIRE, ENGLAND

(ERNIE *and* AGNES *mucking out the cow shed with pitch forks.*)

> SFX - MUSIC
>
> UP TO MIGHTY LONDON
> CAME AN IRISHMAN ONE DAY.
> AS THE STREETS ARE PAVED WITH GOLD
> SURE, EVERYONE WAS GAY,
> SINGING SONGS OF PICCADILLY,
> STRAND AND LEICESTER SQUARE,
> TILL PADDY GOT EXCITED,
> THEN HE SHOUTED TO THEM THERE: (*Fade as* ERNIE *takes over singing.*)

ERNIE *It's a long way to Tipperary, It's a long way to go.*
It's a long way to Tipperary, To the sweetest girl I know!
Goodbye, Piccadilly, Farewell, Leicester Square!
It's a long, long way to Tipperary, But my heart's right there

AGNES Imagine young soldiers singing their hearts out on the way to their deaths on a battlefield.

ERNIE They need to sing to keep their spirits up, don't they? I do that here!

AGNES I wonder what the passengers sang on the Lusitania when it got torpedoed last year?

ERNIE Poor buggars, didn't have time to know what hit them, let alone break out in song. Bloody Germans – sank the unsinkable.

AGNES They said the Titanic was unsinkable too, and the German's had nowt to do with that one.

ERNIE Me-dad says the Titanic was no great loss – with all them rich toffs.

AGNES At least them toffs got to enjoy the good life before they—

ERNIE	They need more Naval ships out in the waters. Forget these ocean liners while we're at war.
AGNES	You'll never catch me crossing an ocean in a tin boat... I'll tell you that for nowt.
ERNIE	I think they're made of steel.
AGNES	Smarty pants! (*Tosses a bit of hay at* ERNIE *with her pitch fork.*)
ERNIE	(*Brushes hay off.*) I'm going to join the navy, like our Gary, when I'm old enough. Then I can help win the war.
AGNES	Giv'over!
ERNIE	(*Back to mucking the hay with pitch fork.*) It better keep going 'til then.
AGNES	You're talking out your arse, Ernie Ogden. I hope it ends tomorrow.
ERNIE	It's only two years in. Me-dad says we're in for the long haul.
AGNES	Your Gary's 19 – you've got three years to wait. It'll be over by then.
ERNIE	Me mate Sam joined up last week! He's only 16 – recruiter didn't care.
AGNES	Well... you just wait 'til they *make* you join. (*Teases.*) Besides, you've never even been on a boat – not even on the Tees. (*Chuckles.*)
ERNIE	No, but I can swim.
AGNES	Then you can rescue them that fall overboard. (*They both laugh.*)
ERNIE	When I join and get sent to sea, I'll write letters to you.
AGNES	Why would I want to read letters about you killing people?

ERNIE · Oh, I won't write about *that*. I'll write to tell you how much I miss you.

AGNES · You won't miss *me*! You'll be too busy keeping your head on your shoulders to stay alive.

ERNIE · (*Stops and stares at* AGNES.) But I love you, Agnes Wimpole.

AGNES · You can't love me! You've only just turned 16. And I'm only 15.

ERNIE · Me-dad married me-Mam when he were 16.

AGNES · Well, they did back then, didn't they? What else was there for 'em to do? And besides, there's a war on now! Nobody's getting wed while the lads are in the trenches.

ERNIE · I'm not in the trenches.

AGNES · No, but mucking out farmer Green's cow shed is just as bad!

ERNIE · Don't you love me?

AGNES · (*Stops. Taken back.*) Love you? I... how... we work together, Ernie, that's all. And we have a laugh – we're mates.

ERNIE · You'll love me when I become a sailor.

AGNES · Well... I do think lads look handsome in a uniform. I've seen them strutting around the Five Lamps.

ERNIE · Oh ya!

AGNES · But I don't want you getting killed parading in enemy waters, just to impress me.

ERNIE · I won't let them krauts kill me.

AGNES · No, you won't!

ERNIE · (*Tries to impress using his pitch fork as a gun.*) I'll shoot them right between the eyes.

AGNES	You couldn't kill a fly, Mister Softy. (*Chuckles*.) And besides, you don't know how to shoot a gun.
ERNIE	(*Excited*.) I'll be on a ship. I won't need to know, will I? We'll fire cannons! Better than those new machine-gun tanks they're using.
AGNES	Silly business… war!
ERNIE	I'm off to play footie on the common tomorrow. Coming to cheer us on?
AGNES	I need to be home to help me-Mam.
ERNIE	We've been working Green's farm all week. Surely she'll give you a full day to yourself.
AGNES	The baby's due next week, isn't it?
ERNIE	Already? That were fast.
AGNES	Tell that to me-Mam. (*Chuckles*.) Eeee, you should see our Gladys, though – so excited, but useless. Me-Mam needs *my* help.
ERNIE	How many's that now – six?
AGNES	Number seven!
ERNIE	I want to have seven babies with you.
AGNES	No bloody way! I won't have time for babies. I'm going to be a dancer.
ERNIE	You've got the legs! (*Whistles*.)
AGNES	(*Excited*.) I'm heading to London.
ERNIE	(*Gobsmacked*.) London? When?
AGNES	Not yet – when war ends.
ERNIE	Crikey, Agnes! How will you be able to—

AGNES	Me Auntie Bea and Uncle Archie live down there and she said she can get me into dance halls.
ERNIE	They have dances up here. Why do you need to go to—?
AGNES	(*Dances around using her pitch fork as a partner.*) London has theatres, Ernie, proper dance halls where they *pay* you to dance. I'll stay with my Auntie just until I start earning a wage.
ERNIE	(*Sad.*) Sounds like you've got it all worked out.
AGNES	I have! (*Starts working the hay again.*) And once I gain a steady position, I'll get me own place.
ERNIE	Live on your own? In London? The Germans are bombing London with their Zeppelins! They'll only be rubble left by the time war ends.
AGNES	Then the Cockneys will be ready for some entertainment, won't they? And goodness knows how many more babies me-Mam will have by then. I'm ready to live somewhere quiet *now*... with a bed of me own.
ERNIE	I'll have to come with you, that's all there is to it.
AGNES	You'll be away, remember, strutting the decks in your naval uniform?
ERNIE	When the war is over, I'll come back.
AGNES	Not everyone comes back, Ernie.
ERNIE	Don't say that!
AGNES	(*Apologetic.*) I don't mean you. You'll always come back to Teesside.
ERNIE	Will *you* be coming back... you know... to see your Mam?
AGNES	Of course.
ERNIE	And you'll write?

AGNES	Every day.
ERNIE	You say that now, but—
AGNES	Well… every week. I'll be busy with all me dance rehearsals, won't I?
ERNIE	Promise?

SFX – BELL RINGS TO MARK THE END OF THE WORK SHIFT

AGNES	(*Exasperated.*) I'm not leaving yet, Ernie – 'cept for here. Longest day ever. (*Tosses her pitchfork in the hay.*) Heck! I hate the stink of cow dung! (*Puts a sweater on.*)
ERNIE	No worse than baby-nappies.
AGNES	(*Shouts out.*) Hurry up, England, and end the war! I can't wait to get out of here and start me dancing career. (*Makes her way to leave.*)
ERNIE	(*Darts in front of her to block her way.*) Come to me game so the lads can see me *leggy* girl.
AGNES	I'm not a trophy for your friends to *ogle* at.
ERNIE	But you are my girlfriend, right Agnes?
AGNES	I'm your friend, who happens to be a girl.
ERNIE	(*Dejected.*) Oh!
AGNES	(*Makes her way to leave.*) Score a goal… for me. Hey, maybe Boro will be looking for a new forward.
ERNIE	(*Resigned.*) I'm not *that* good!
AGNES	Sure you are! Good luck in the match, Ernie. (EXITS.)
ERNIE	(*To himself.*) Not feeling particularly lucky right now. (*Tosses pitchfork in hay.*) London! Bloody hell! (EXITS.)

(TRANSITION)

OCTOBER 1920

HAMMERSMITH PALAIS DANCE HALL, LONDON, ENGLAND

(AGNES *sits at a table, sullen, nursing a drink.* RODNEY *in his British soldier's uniform, stares at* AGNES *from across the room.*)

    SFX – DANCE HALL MUSIC

RODNEY	(*Comes up to* AGNES *from behind.*) You've had your hands caressing that glass for over 30 minutes, Hen. Why not wrap them around me on the dance floor instead?
AGNES	Is that the best you can do for an opening line?
RODNEY	Did it work?
AGNES	It's a bit forward.
RODNEY	Can I join you?
AGNES	(*Starts to notice him.*) It's a free country! Isn't that what you fought for?
RODNEY	I did fight for it – and won it – just for you.
AGNES	Just for me, eh?
RODNEY	Aye! (*Sits down opposite her.*)
AGNES	You don't even know me!
RODNEY	Well, let's start there, then, shall we? I'm Rodney. Private Rodney Macdonald.
AGNES	A Macdonald, eh? Glasgow?
RODNEY	Naire a Glasgie, Hen. Galashiels!
AGNES	I'm Agnes – of Thornaby-on-Tees.
RODNEY	I thought I detected a Yorkie. I'm very pleased to meet you, Agnes-of-Thornaby.

AGNES (*Pause.*) So...?

RODNEY Why the long face?

AGNES Oh, you are full of compliments.

RODNEY You got me wrong. You have a face that shines, like a summer's day. But it's presently behind a cloud, isn't it, now?

AGNES (*Big sigh.*) Not that it's any of your business... but... I didn't get chosen at me dance audition this aft.

RODNEY Is that all?

AGNES Is that all? I've been here nine months and I haven't been chosen once. And if I have to keep working for the Twat family... I'll just burst.

RODNEY (*Laughing.*) The *Twat* family?

AGNES (*Laughing.*) That's not their real name – just what we staff call them. I help with the housekeeping and child-mind their little... buggers – but... just until I get me first break as a professional dancer.

RODNEY So you were all set to dance today, then?

AGNES Yes, well... for my audition.

RODNEY And yet here you sit, at the Hammersmith Palais Dance Hall... and *not* dancing.

AGNES I came with me friend Pauline. (*Points.*) But... she's dumped me to go chat-up that bloke over there.

RODNEY So it's a partner replacement you're after?

AGNES I don't blame her, though. I haven't been the best company for our weekly nights' out.

RODNEY Well, let me oblige you then, Agnes-of-Thornaby.

AGNES With what?

RODNEY   A dance, you so desire.

AGNES   I don't know.

RODNEY   (*Breaks into song with a lovely voice that captivates* AGNES.)

If my true love, she were gone, I would surely find another, Where wild mountain thyme, Grows around the blooming heather, Will ye go lassie, go?

AGNES   (*Coy.*) We've only just met!

RODNEY   Aye! There's no better way to get to know each other than a shuffle on the dance floor.

AGNES   Alright. But only a fast song, mind.

RODNEY   Only a fast song? But of course – I insist! What kind of spiv do you take me fer?

         SFX – DANCE MUSIC SWELLS UP

AGNES   (*Chuckles. Takes his hand and stands.*) A soldier with a glib tongue.

RODNEY   How's this tempo, me-lady? To your satisfaction?

AGNES   (*Chuckles.*) It should keep your hands at bay. Me-Mam warmed me about lads like you.

RODNEY   (*Starts to dance with* AGNES *but they are both engaged with each other's company and are just moving not in time with the music.*) Nay, a lad, anymore, Hen. That's what war does to you. Them that starts it takes young innocents, like me, puts a gun in their hands, and ships us off to foreign lands to fight other brainwashed lads… in a *different* uniform.

AGNES   I think war is horrible.

RODNEY   Aye, it is that, Hen. It can get bloody ugly. But… we survived.

AGNES   Will you be leaving the army then, now it's over?

RODNEY   That was just Europe's war. There's unrest all around the world. I'm only just back from Africa, and now they want to ship me off to India.

AGNES   Surely they can use their *own* people to fight their *own* battles.

RODNEY   Britain still wants her own soldiers in her colonies. Protecting what they *think* is theirs. (*Chuckles.*)

AGNES   When are you off then… to India?

RODNEY   Monday.

AGNES   Crikey, *you've* thrown your hat in the ring… for someone so young.

RODNEY   I've been sent to three different countries since I joined up three years ago.

AGNES   For how long? I mean, how long will you be in India?

RODNEY   A few weeks for a start, then I'll be back home for a wee while… for Christmas.

AGNES   In Scotland?

RODNEY   Unless there's something to keep me here… in London.

AGNES   (*Coy*) Well, I can't think of what that would be.

RODNEY   Or *who* that could be?

AGNES   (*Smiling.*) Do you have someone… in Scotland?

RODNEY   Me-Mam & dad – James and Angus – my two younger brothers.

AGNES   Eeee, you can't get more Scottish than that.

RODNEY   Ummm…. the Campbell's may have an opposing view on that. (*Chuckles.*)

AGNES   I meant, is there someone back in Scotland that you're... *sweet* on?

RODNEY   No, Hen. I think London has all the sweets I'm looking for. (*Takes her hand and twirls her closer to him.*)

(TRANSITION.)

1921

ONE SPOTLIGHT ON RODNEY IN INDIA AND A 2ND SPOTLIGHT ON AGNES IN ENGLAND, BOTH AT A TABLE READING OR WRITING LETTERS

RODNEY   (*Writes letter.*) Dear Agnes,

Roses are red, violets are blue
All I want, is for me and you
To be together, no matter the weather
Kissing the time away.

Congratulations on your chorus role in *The Rebel Maid*. I knew it wouldn't be long before you were successful. You've got the legs! Hope the Empire's full every night to enjoy your talent. Well done! Rodney.

AGNES   (*Reads letter from* RODNEY.) My dearest Agnes,

Memories of my leave, still sing in my head,
five whole days so rare.
Dancing 'til dawn, what were the chances?
All those exquisite *slow* dances!

(*Sings, but not very well.*) *And we'll all go together, To pluck wild mountain thyme, All around the blooming heather, Will ye go lassie, go?*
So looking forward to seeing you again in a few weeks. Your Rodney.

1922

RODNEY   (*Writes letter.*) My dearest Aggie,

How I wish we could be together
Every day and every night,
Tasting the wonder of your lips forever
Then all in my world will be right.

Lady of the Rose sounds like the perfect role for you. And dance captain to boot. Congratulations, Aggie, Luv. I'll be back in time for your opening. Love from your greatest admirer, Roddy.

AGNES (*Reads letter from* RODNEY.) My dearest Aggie,

We danced upon the midnight clear
A Christmas to remember
The stars shone down on your lovely face
All in the sweet December.

(*Sigh!*) All my love, Roddy.

FEBRUARY 1923

RODNEY (*With a pint in his hand, writes letter.*) My dearest Aggie, I'll be back in London on a five day leave in a couple of weeks. Hope you can book some time off from your show. I can't wait to see you because, as blunt as this may sound – I have a question to put to you – a very important question. I realize it's un-romantic, but here it goes… Agnes Wimpole, will you marry me? Let your answer be a resounding yes, and make me the happiest Scot on the planet.

AGNES (*Writes letter.*) Dear Mam and Dad, I have the most brilliant news! Roddy and I are getting married. Can you contact the vicar for February 26? I know it's not much time, but that's when Roddy's back in the U.K. We need a hotel room booked for our wedding night, too. Aunt Bea and Uncle Archie are accompanying me the day before. They'll need a room booked for a couple of nights, as well. Can you make it a different hotel? (*Chuckles with embarrassment.*) Ask Gladys if she would be me Maid of Honour. I can't wait for you to meet him. And I'm certain you'll fall in love with him almost as much as me. I'm so excited. I'm going to be Agnes Macdonald.

April 1923

RODNEY (*Lies on an army cot, writes a letter.*) You're having a baby? Our wedding night was magical but I didn't realize just how much until I read your recent letter. My darling Aggie, I'm bursting at the seams. I've been a little under the weather and pinned to the medic ward for the past few days. Nothing serious... so I'll just have to give it time. I want to hear all about your swelling belly. I'm almost finished here. My tour is up in June. Then we will be together forever. All my love, my darling Aggie. Yours for always, Roddy.

June 1923

AGNES (*Writes letter.*) Dear Mam and Dad, Just a quick note. I'm over the morning sickness now. But I had to leave my show as I was missing too many rehearsals. But I'm not upset. I'm too excited about having me baby. Roddy's not well. They're keeping him in India until he's healthy enough to transport back to London. I'm quite worried. I know we planned to come north this month, but with Roddy not back yet, we'll postpone to August. Still not too close to baby's due date in November, so let's plan on that.

October 1923

RODNEY (*Lies on an army cot and dictates letter.*) My darling Aggie. You'll notice that the handwriting is different in this letter. I'm dictating to my nurse, for her to put my words on paper. I'm glad to hear you've gone back home to Thornaby to be with your Mam and Dad. Things aren't looking too good, Hen. I have, apparently, caught some wretched disease here and they're having difficulty containing it. The doc will arrange transport home to London as soon as I'm well enough to travel.

AGNES (*Continues to read the letter, crying.*) I don't want you to worry. They're hoping the doctors in the UK will have more advanced treatments to stop this thing in its tracks. Or, should I say, my liver. I will have the field office contact you as soon as I leave, to let you know when I'm back in London. It won't be long now, Aggie, Luv. I might even be back in time for our baby's birth. Love you more than you will ever know. Forever, your Roddy. (*Big cry.*)

(TRANSITION)

EARLY DECEMBER 1923

LONDON MILITARY HOSPITAL ROOM

(RODNEY *in a hospital bed.* ENTER AGNES *with baby in her arms.*)

AGNES (*Shocked at the sight of* RODNEY.) Eeee, Roddy, Luv! What have they—

RODNEY (*Weak.*) Don't be afraid, Hen.

AGNES Is it safe to come in?

RODNEY (*Weak.*) Aye. Come closer so I can see your beautiful face.

AGNES (*Slowly walks towards the bed.*) I... (*Takes a big breath, fights back the tears and tries to be cheerful.*) Here we go, little one. Come meet your Da-da.

RODNEY (*Weak.*) Aren't you a sight for sore eyes.

AGNES We have a daughter, Roddy – a beautiful baby girl.

RODNEY A daughter! Just what I was hoping for. When was she born?

AGNES November 10th. I... I had no idea how to contact you 'til I arrived back at Aunt Bea's yesterday. She had the telegram from your field commander.

RODNEY I just arrived four days ago, meself.

AGNES Wh... what do the doctors say? They can get you well again, right? They can fix—

RODNEY Let's not waste our time talking about that, Hen. Let me see our wee bairn. (*Struggles to sit up.*)

AGNES I haven't named her yet. I... wanted to wait until... Do you want to hold her? (*Handing baby over to* RODNEY.)

RODNEY (*Weak.*) Oh, I do, Hen. More than you know. But... I think it best just to look on, for now – just in case.

AGNES   (*Retreats baby back to her body.*) Let me unravel her blanket so you can have a good look, then.

RODNEY   (*Struggles to stretch over to see her.*) Oh, Aggie, she's a right Bobby Dazzler.

AGNES   I think she looks like you. I mean… when you were well.

RODNEY   Oh, no, Hen, she has her mother's beauty – as beautiful as a flower. (*Looks down at baby.*) Can we call her… Violet?

AGNES   Violet… it's a perfect name for her.

RODNEY   Well there you have it, my little Petal. Violet Macdonald. May your life be filled with joy and your heart filled with love. And e'er you find yourself with neither, you can borrow… *and* keep, what overflows from mine… at this moment… and forever more. (*Sings with a struggle.*) *And we'll all go together, To pluck wild mountain thyme, All around the blooming Violet, Will ye go lassie, go?* (*AGNES wipes the tears from her cheek.*)

(TRANSITION)

MARCH 1924

FRONT ROOM OF AGNES'S FAMILY HOME IN THORNABY

(AGNES *folds laundry.* VIOLET *is asleep in a wee cot.*)

AGNES   Ay-up, look what the cat dragged in. (*Looks off stage. Pause.*) Well, don't just stand there like a piece of furniture, Ernie, come in.

ERNIE   (*Off.*) If that's alright.

AGNES   Well, you're here now.

ERNIE   (ENTERS. *Hesitant.*) Hello, Agnes, Luv. You're looking well.

AGNES   Am I? Huh!

ERNIE   Considering what... I ran into your Mam yesterday... at the market.

AGNES   She never said.

ERNIE   She told me... what happened and that you were back home. I... I... I'm so sorry you had to go through that.

AGNES   (*Hardens.*) I'm sorry too. (*Pause.*) Me-Mam wrote and told me about your Gary. I was sad to hear about him... you know, getting himself killed.

ERNIE   He survived the whole bloody war – fought in four battles and then... gets himself killed in silly war-game exercises, here at home.

AGNES   Just like your Gar, though, eh? Taking bloody risks, going all in... for the win. And gave it all up... for what?

ERNIE   Me-Mam was beside herself – still is, really. And me-Dad... well...he's not been the same since.

AGNES   (*There is a long pause.*) Still working at the market, then? Or did Boro pick you up and the market just keeps you busy in the off season? (*Chuckles.*)

Blooming Violet

ERNIE	No. (*Embarrassed.*) At the market. (*Optimistic.*) But there's some better paying jobs as a riveter opening at the shipyards next month. I'll be applying there.
AGNES	What happened with all your *joining-the-Royal-Navy* dreams?
ERNIE	Well… with our Gar and… well, me-Mam still needed me around, didn't she, so…
AGNES	You were smart not to join, Ernie. War, it's… just hell on earth.
ERNIE	(*Optimistic.*) Yes, but… it's well over now, so I'm better suited to stay close to home… you know, where I'm needed.
AGNES	Your Mam was… she were wise to keep you close by. Not send you off to foreign lands where… God only knows… (*Pause.*) Or joining up at all, for that matter!
ERNIE	(*Tries to change the mood.*) So… is that… is she… Violet?
AGNES	(*Goes over to baby* VIOLET. *Softens.*) Yes, this is our Violet.
ERNIE	She's so tiny.
AGNES	No she's not! She's perfect.
ERNIE	No, I don't mean in a bad way. I mean, she's… she's lovely, Agnes.
AGNES	She's four months old already.
ERNIE	I'm sorry about what happened… with your man, an' all.
AGNES	You have nowt to be sorry about. You didn't kill him! Not even killed in battle – just caught some poisonous disease from dirty foreign lands … (*Pause.*) He… Roddy died on New Years' Eve – just before midnight.
ERNIE	Can I… I mean… is it alright if I hold her?
AGNES	She's sleeping, but sure. (*Picks up* VIOLET *and hands to* ERNIE.) Careful now!

ERNIE	Oh, Agnes. She's the spittin' image of you – a right Bobby Dazzler.
AGNES	(*Softening*.) That's what Rod... yes she is.
ERNIE	Are you staying here, then? You know... until... or back to London?
AGNES	(*Despondent*.) There's nowt in London for me now.
ERNIE	What about your dancing? Your Mam said that you'd been having some good success—
AGNES	Me dancing career is over, Ernie. I'm in no fit shape now to—
ERNIE	You'll soon be back—
AGNES	I'm not sure where I'm going to end up, if truth be told. It's been grand to be with our Gladys again, mind. She loves helping out with our Violet, but it's crowded here, with me-Mam, Dad – *and* six others.
ERNIE	What about the other five? (*Chuckles*.)
AGNES	Well, they moved out, didn't they? No room. Except our Danny – he died of TB last year.
ERNIE	Oh for crissakes, Ernie Ogden, shut yer gob.
AGNES	It's alright. You weren't to know.
ERNIE	I'm sorry to hear that, about wee Danny-boy.
AGNES	Me-Mam insisted that I come back here with our Violet. (*Holding back tears*.) How am I going...? I only have a pittance with an army widow's pension and a wee—
ERNIE	I can't imagine what you're going through, Luv.
AGNES	Nobody can.
ERNIE	It's hardened you – I can see that.

Blooming Violet

AGNES   (*Defensive.*) Do you blame me?

ERNIE   No, Agnes! Not one bit. But… my heart is breaking… seeing you like this – and with this wee one taking in your anger.

AGNES   I don't regret having her, if that's what you're saying! (*Goes to take* VIOLET *back.*)

ERNIE   (*Steps back with* VIOLET.) No, no! Agnes, Luv, I'm not saying that at all. But… what you're going through… I mean how you're feeling… well…

AGNES   I don't mean to be like this, Ernie, but I feel… stuck, trapped… alone!

ERNIE   Well, I… I have a suggestion – if you'll hear me out.

AGNES   At this point I'm open to almost anything. (*Looks at* VIOLET.)

ERNIE   (*Puts baby back in cot.*) Let me put you down here, Petal.

AGNES   Careful…

ERNIE   There you go. Now… (*Gets down on one knee.*) Agnes Wimpole—

AGNES   Oh, for crissakes, Ernie – stop right there!

ERNIE   Sorry! Macdonald – Agnes Macdonald.

AGNES   No Ernie, that's not it.

ERNIE   You said you were open to—

AGNES   I can't marry you.

ERNIE   Why not?

AGNES   I won't be your pity case – wedded out of pity.

ERNIE   Hardly pity, Luv. I already have a ring for you. (*Fumbles in his pocket.*)

AGNES   You have a ring? You only just found out I were back!

ERNIE   Agnes, I've had this ring for years. (*Stands up*.) I've only just finished paying for it.

AGNES   But I was already… Oh, Ernie. I'm sorry if—

ERNIE   I love you, Agnes. Always have and always will.

AGNES   But I don't… it wouldn't be fair – to you – or to me!

ERNIE   I love you enough for the both of us. And in time… maybe… maybe you'll come to return my affections—

AGNES   But I… I have Violet, now.

ERNIE   Yes you do. And I will promise you this… I will raise this wee bairn as if she were me own. For she's your child, Agnes, and my love extends to all of you… and that includes Violet.

AGNES   Oh, Ernie, what are we to do with you?

ERNIE   Just… just give us a chance, Luv.

AGNES   I don't know what to say.

ERNIE   Say *yes*, Agnes. *Please*, say yes!

AGNES   (*She picks up* VIOLET.) What do *you* say Violet? (*Looks at* ERNIE. *Pause.*) I… I guess we say… yes. (*Weak smile.*) We say yes.

(TRANSITION.)

May, 1932

FRONT ROOM OF AGNES AND ERNIE'S ROW HOUSE IN THORNABY

(AGNES *and* VIOLET *are sitting on a settee.*)

AGNES (*Rocks baby in arms.*) Violet, Luv, can you fetch me a nappy off the line? I think our Maureen needs a change.

VIOLET Yes, Mam. (*Stands up.*)

AGNES And can you check on your brother. He's been out playing footie the whole morning.

VIOLET (*Leaves room.*) Mrs. Mussum won't be happy with Malcolm pounding his ball against her back fence. You know how she gets.

AGNES He's playing with her son, Peter, so she can give them both an earful, if she's got a mind. But that ball-banging is nowt compared to the shouting and knocking about we hear through these thin walls.

VIOLET (*Off.*) Only when their dad's home.

AGNES Anyway, let's get our Malcolm in before she marches him over here taking the high and mighty with me. Time for his tea, anyway.

VIOLET (*Off. Shouts.*) Malcolm! Enough, now. Mam says it's tea-time. (*Door slams. Enters with nappy.*) What *is* for tea?

AGNES I'm not sure, Luv. There's not much left until your dad's pay packet. Not two ha'pennies to rub together until then.

VIOLET I can skim the fat and green bits from last week's stew. Maybe add a few more cups of water so it'll go around.

AGNES I've already watered it down, Luv. (*Big sigh.*) We can't be living like this. They've cut back your dad's shifts at the shipyard again and I know it's the depression and all, but this is not right. I need to help bring in some wages.

VIOLET You could be a dancer again, Mam!

AGNES	No, Luv. Those days are over for me. (*Reflective*.) Barely got started.
VIOLET	What doing, then?
AGNES	I've heard there are some domestic jobs, over on the Manager Estates that pay a fair wage – just a few hours a week, mind, until we can get on top of things.
VIOLET	Oh, Mam that would be grand. But… who will look after *us*? Aunty Gladys?
AGNES	She's working now, Luv. I was thinking… *you* could, Violet. You're very capable.
VIOLET	Giv'over – I'm only eight.
AGNES	Eight and a half, Luv. You'll be nine in November. You've been helping with our Malcolm and Maureen since the days they were born. You know how to take care of them. And Malcolm… he's already six.
VIOLET	Would I be allowed?
AGNES	It'd be only after school. I… umm… I could ask Mrs. Mussum next door to keep an eye on things… in case of an emergency.
VIOLET	Oh, 'eck! Not sure I want her bossing us about. Besides, she has her own five to look after. And they're a handful in of themselves.
AGNES	Just for an emergency – hopefully her sorry arse won't need to darken our doorway, but in an emergency she'll be fine. And maybe we can take in some washing – we could do that together on the weekends, Luv.
VIOLET	What will daddy say?
AGNES	If he's honest, I think he'll be glad of the help.
VIOLET	Here's our Maureen's nappy.
AGNES	You change her, Violet, Luv. Get some practice in.

ERNIE	(ENTERS.) Eeee, it's good to be home. Give us a cuddle with that wee bairn. (*Takes* MAUREEN *in his arms.*)
AGNES	Any luck?
VIOLET	Mam's going to find work.
ERNIE	What?
AGNES	Violet, I'll tell him.
ERNIE	You don't need to work, Agnes.
AGNES	I want to, Ernie. The burden shouldn't be all on you. Not in these times.
ERNIE	What about our Malcolm and Maureen? And our Violet?
AGNES	Well, I thought… maybe… Violet could help mind them—
ERNIE	But she's only—
AGNES	Just part time – after school. We're drowning here. And many of the other Mams are taking jobs outside the home. Mrs. Mussum does the washing for three other families—
VIOLET	All those stranger's knickers and underpants flung over her back wall and gate for all and sundry to see— (*Chuckles.*)
ERNIE	I'll not have—
AGNES	Just until we get on track, Luv. Violet and I can do this.
ERNIE	It's not right. People will think I can't provide for you all.
AGNES	(*Stern.*) Who cares what other people think. They can stick their oar… where the sun don't shine. You can't help that they're cutting down on your shifts.
VIOLET	And you're not a *bloody* loser like Mr.—
ERNIE	Eeee 'eck… watch your mouth, little Miss. (*Chuckles.*)
VIOLET	A *loser*, like Mr. Mussum… spends most of his time in the pub after work.

Blooming Violet

AGNES	(*Chuckles.*) Where did you hear that? (*Takes* MAUREEN.)
ERNIE	Their son, Peter, right?
VIOLET	He hates his father.
AGNES	Mrs. Mussum says the bastard beats Peter if he gets in his way.
VIOLET	And Peter says his dad slaps his Mam about when he's had a few!
ERNIE	The man doesn't deserve a family.
VIOLET	I bet they wish they had a daddy like you. (*Gives* ERNIE *a hug.*)
AGNES	That lad will grow bigger than his dad, soon enough, and then he'll get what he truly deserves.
ERNIE	Now you've got the vote, Luv, maybe you can choose a politician who'll work *for* the people and get blokes like Mussum locked up.
AGNES	They won't be spouting promises like that on their soapboxes. They'll lose all the men vote.
ERNIE	Not mine! But you're probably right. It's them that are popular who gets in anyway.
AGNES	And money and connections is what gets them popular. Out for themselves, the lot of them!
ERNIE	Just not having me usual luck on the geegees, these days, Luv.
AGNES	We'll be fine, Ernie.
ERNIE	I've tried me best to provide for you, Agnes.
AGNES	I know you have, Luv. I know.
VIOLET	I don't mind, daddy. If it helps, I don't mind, really.

ERNIE	We are truly blessed. (*Hugs* VIOLET *and* AGNES.)
AGNES	(*Efficient.*) Now, let's get that nappy of Maureen's changed.
VIOLET	I can do it, Mam. (*Takes* MAUREEN *from* AGNES.) Come on, wee Maureen. Time to get you cleaned up. (ERNIE *proudly watches* VIOLET *with baby.* AGNES *watches on with a weak smile.*)

(TRANSITION.)

SEPTEMBER 1939

THE POSH DINING ROOM OF MR. & MRS. ASHTON

(VIOLET *on her knees, finishes scrubbing the floor.*)

VIOLET (*Sings.*) *Just whistle while you work* (*Whistles.*)
And cheerfully together we
Can tidy up this place.

Do-do-do-do-do-do-do. (*Whistles.*)
It won't take long when there's a song
To help you set the pace. Ta-dah! (*Tosses her scrubbing brush into a bucket of water.*) Well, that's me done for the day. I should make it home for our Maureen's birthday cake.

MRS. ASHTON (ENTER. *Shadow of* MRS. ASHTON *is seen. Off.*) Where is your sister?

VIOLET (*Startled.*) Oh! I didn't hear you come in. (*Stands and gathers up her cleaning supplies.*) It's her birthday today, Mrs. Ashton, so she went straight home after school with our Malcolm.

MRS. ASHTON (*Shadow of* MRS. ASHTON *is seen. Off.*) Well, that's unfortunate.

VIOLET Pardon me?

MRS. ASHTON (*Shadow of* MRS. ASHTON *is seen. Off.*) With this new war situation, Mr. Ashton and myself feel obliged to do our part. So we are hosting a very important soirée tomorrow evening with people... well, you wouldn't be acquainted with... and, of course, requires that our crystal-ware be sparkling.

VIOLET Oh, I'm finished for the day, now, Mrs. Ashton. I need to get home.

MRS. ASHTON (*Shadow of* MRS. ASHTON *is seen. Off.*) But you're not finished, are you my dear?

VIOLET I did all what you wrote down - floors, linens, washing, dusting, polishing – I've been here a full eight hours.

MRS. ASHTON	(*Shadow of* MRS. ASHTON *is seen. Off.*) I suppose I forgot to *add* the crystal.
VIOLET	Yes, you must have.
MRS. ASHTON	(*Shadow of* MRS. ASHTON *is seen. Off.*) If your sister was here, you could have gotten your duties completed earlier and had time for the crystal.
VIOLET	Our Maureen's only just turned eight. Today! And *you* don't pay her. I give her a couple of pence out of me wages. It's just convenient for her to come here after school.
MRS. ASHTON	(*Shadow of* MRS. ASHTON *is seen. Off.*) Aren't you a generous big sister? But still, I require my crystal to be washed, dried and put away. Am I making myself clear?
VIOLET	Oh, yes, but I'm finished for the day. (*Gathers up her coat and belongings.*) I'll take me week's wages now, if you don't mind, Mrs. Ashton.
MRS. ASHTON	(*Shadow of* MRS. ASHTON *is seen. Off.*) Wages? You haven't finished to *my* satisfaction, to earn your weekly wage.
VIOLET	I worked this whole week! I did all what you asked. I didn't even take me full dinner break on two of those days so I could get your whole—
MRS. ASHTON	(*Shadow of* MRS. ASHTON *is seen. Off.*) Almost done then aren't you, my dear. The crystal won't take long – only a dozen glasses. Oh, and the water goblets, mustn't forget the water goblets. I'll prepare your pay packet for when you've completed the task at hand. And *do* take care, won't you, my dear. These glasses are very delicate and are worth more than you will ever know. (EXITS.)
VIOLET	Why, that... (*Starts to tear up. Thrashes her coat on the floor.*) She can't make me do this. Why is she making me do this? (*Takes a crystal glass from the cupboard.*) Worth more than... I should just smash the lot of them! That'd teach her!

MR. ASHTON	(ENTER. *Shadow of* MR. ASHTON *is seen. Off.*) On your own today, my dear?
VIOLET	(*Startled.*) Aaaah!
MR. ASHTON	(*Shadow of* MR. ASHTON. *Off.*) Are you alright?
VIOLET	(*Nervous.*) You startled me, Mr. Ashton. That's all.
MR. ASHTON	(*Shadow of* MR. ASHTON. *Off.*) Where's that wee one of yours?
VIOLET	(*Cautious.*) My sister's already home.
MR. ASHTON	(*Shadow of* MR. ASHTON. *Off.*) So just the two of us, then?
VIOLET	(*Cautious.*) Yes. Well no! Mrs. Ashton is still here.
MR. ASHTON	(*Shadow of* MR. ASHTON. *Off.*) She's busy in the parlour. We won't disturb her.
VIOLET	(*Nervous.*) I really must get started on this crystal, Mr. Ashton, as I need to get home. It's me sister's birthday.
MR. ASHTON	(*Shadow of* MR. ASHTON *coming closer. Off.*) Oh, yes, you will be in a hurry, my dear. So, maybe, *I* could help you.
VIOLET	(*Nervous.*) No! I'm fine. I can do it on me own. (*Picks up a rag and starts to wipe the glass.*)
MR. ASHTON	(*Shadow of* MR. ASHTON. *Off.*) Don't be silly. An extra pair of hands—
VIOLET	(*Firm.*) I don't want your hands. I... I... I just want to get this done so I can go home.
MR. ASHTON	(*Shadow of* MR. ASHTON *comes close. Off.*) Are you playing with me, little Miss?
VIOLET	No! I.. I need to finish up and get to me sister's birthday party.
MR. ASHTON	(*Shadow of* MR. ASHTON *comes close. Off.*) A *party* you say. Is that what you want? A party? Well, now you *are* flirting with me.

VIOLET	(*Backs up.*) No! Please. Leave me... to get on with your *precious* crystal.
MR. ASHTON	(*Shadow of* MR. ASHTON *comes even closer. Off. Laughing.*) I like *our* little party, don't you?
VIOLET	You're scaring me, Mr. Ashton!
MR. ASHTON	(*Shadow of* MR. ASHTON *comes even closer. Off.*) And you... you're always teasing me, you little vixen. What is it that you want from me, girl?
VIOLET	(*Backs up further.*) Nothing. I... I... I don't want anything—
MR. ASHTON	(*Shadow of* MR. ASHTON *makes a motion to drop his pants. Off.*) I can finish the crystal if you come over here and... pleasure me.
VIOLET	(*Drops crystal glass.*) Oh no! Look what you made me do. (Mr. ASHTON EXITS.) It's smashed into a million— (*retrieves broom and begins to sweep the glass.*) Oh 'eck!
MRS. ASHTON	(ENTER. *Shadow of* MRS. ASHTON *appears. Off.*) What have you done?
VIOLET	(*Picking up pieces off the floor.*) I... I... I'm sorry, Mrs. Ashton. Truly I am. It was an accident. It slipped from me hand—
MRS. ASHTON	(*Shadow of* MRS. ASHTON. *Off.*) You spiteful child! You broke my crystal on purpose.
VIOLET	No! I would never... please Mrs. Ashton. It... it... it was Mr. Ashton.
MRS. ASHTON	(*Shadow of* MRS. ASHTON. *Off.*) You're blaming my husband?
VIOLET	Not directly, no. But he—
MRS. ASHTON	(*Shadow of* MRS. ASHTON. *Off.*) You leave me no choice, child. This week's wages will be withheld in order to cover the replacement cost of my broken crystal.
VIOLET	(*Stands.*) You can't do that!

MRS. ASHTON	(*Shadow of* MRS. ASHTON. *Off*.) Can I not? Don't be impertinent! Your meager wages still won't cover the cost.
VIOLET	But I worked all week—
MRS. ASHTON	(*Shadow of* MRS. ASHTON. *Off*.) This will teach you to be more careful with other people's belongings in the future.
VIOLET	(*Grabs her coat and races out the door*.) It's not fair. It's not…

SHADOW DISAPPEARS. VIOLET IS RUNNING HOME, EXHAUSTED AND CRYING. SHE ENTERS THE FRONT ROOM OF HER HOME.

(ERNIE *picks up and folds used newspaper gift-wrapping*.)

AGNES	(ENTERS.) I've just had to retrieve our Timmy from the hen-coop again. (*Chuckles*.)
ERNIE	He's quite fond of them.
AGNES	Best not let him get too fond. One of them will be featured on our Sunday dinner table very soon.
ERNIE	He's a ways from being able to count. (*Chuckles*.) Hopefully, he won't notice.
AGNES	(ENTER VIOLET, *out of breath*.) There you are! Running late today, of all days. You're just in time for our Maureen's cake.
ERNIE	Everyone's out back playing with her new toys.
AGNES	Next door gave their Peggy's old pony stick.
ERNIE	Our Maureen doesn't care it's been used. She always played on it when she were over there. She were over the moon to receive it as a gift.
AGNES	(*Notices* VIOLET's *distraught state*.) Everything alright, Luv?
ERNIE	You needn't be upset for missing part of the birthday. She'll be thrilled that you're—
VIOLET	(*Trying to get the words*.) That woman… I hate that woman.

AGNES	Mrs. Ashton?
VIOLET	(*Upset.*) Oh, Mam! She won't pay me wages for the week.
ERNIE	What you talking about? She can't do that!
AGNES	You were there every day – and on time. You're a good worker.
VIOLET	A… a…. and Mr. Ashton! Mr. Ashton came…
AGNES	(*Concerned.*) Go on.
VIOLET	He were saying… bad things… I got scared…I broke a crystal glass… and Mrs. Ashton said she needed me wages to replace the cost… I didn't mean it… I'm usually so careful with her—
ERNIE	What did Mr. Ashton do, *exactly*?
VIOLET	(*Embarrassed.*) It's what he wanted… *me* to do.
AGNES	I'll give him what for. You never mind, Violet. (*Grabs her coat.*) I'll get your wages.
ERNIE	(*Angry.*) I'm coming with you, Luv. (*Grabs his coat.*) I won't have a bloke – and I don't care how much his bloody crystal's worth – messing with our Violet.
AGNES	Wipe your face Violet, Luv, and join the others in the yard. And keep an eye on our Timmy.
ERNIE	(*Determined.*) We'll be back soon *with* your wages—
AGNES	And then some!
VIOLET	I'm not going back there – to the Ashton's. I'm never going—
ERNIE	Oh, I know, Luv. They'll not see you in the vicinity of their *stench* ever again. Mark my words.
AGNES	They won't be able to see much of anything by the time I'm finished with them both! (*Grabs a rolling pin and storms out.*)

ERNIE	Put the candles on the cake, Luv and go play with the others.
AGNES	We won't be long. (ERNIE *and* AGNES EXIT.)
VIOLET	(VIOLET *wipes away her tears and takes a deep breath. Puts a fake smile on her face.*) Right, where's the birthday girl?

(TRANSITION.)

AUGUST 1940

FRONT ROOM OF AGNES AND ERNIE'S HOME IN THORNABY

(VIOLET, *with her hand covering her swollen face sits at* AGNES'S *feet.* AGNES *sits on a chair stroking* VIOLET's *hair.*)

    SFX - AIR RAID SIREN.

AGNES	Damn war! I need to close the bloody drapes again. (*Stands and closes drapes.*) Now don't you be worrying about what the dentist said, Luv. Everybody's gums bleed once in awhile. How were we to know?
VIOLET	(*Mumbles.*) Why me?
AGNES	Poison pyorrhea has afflicted a few around these parts. It can travel through the whole body... your teeth *had* to come out, Luv – to save your life!
VIOLET	It still hurts.
AGNES	I know, Luv. (*Big sigh.*) I'll tell you what, you're just coming up to your 17th birthday and I have some extra money, so we'll use it get you new teeth.
VIOLET	(*Mumbles.*) Where did you get—
AGNES	You needn't know any details, Luv. I can do anything when I put me mind to it.
VIOLET	(*Mumbles.*) Oh Mam!
AGNES	You have your whole life ahead of you. And for that, you'll need new teeth.
VIOLET	(*Mumbles.*) Lads won't want a saggy-faced lass.
AGNES	Plenty of time for lads and the heartache that comes with it, Luv. We just have to wait for your mouth to heal.
VIOLET	(*Mumbles.*) I can still taste the blood.

AGNES	We'll replace the gauze before bed. The bleeding should stop by morning. And then, in a few months—
VIOLET	(*Shouts.*) A few months! Ow! (*Comforts her mouth.*)
AGNES	(*Sits back down to comfort* VIOLET.) Mind yourself, Luv. You don't want the stitches to come away. (*Breaks down in tears.*)
	SFX – AIR RAID SIREN STOPS
VIOLET	(*Mumbles.*) Don't cry, Mam! I'm sorry. (*Wipes her tears away.*) I'll be fine.
AGNES	(*Sniff.*) I know, Luv. Maybe play your piano – it'll take your mind off—
VIOLET	(*Mumbles.*) I don't want to.
AGNES	It was good of our Gladys to give it to you.
VIOLET	(*Mumbles.*) It doesn't play right. That's why she got rid.
AGNES	Now, Violet! We'll have none of that. Let's not be ungrateful. Just because… Look, why don't I put kettle on and we'll have a cuppa?
ERNIE	(ENTERS.) Hello, Luv. (*Gives a peck on* AGNES'S *cheek.*) Everything alright? (*Wipes a tear from her cheek.*)
AGNES	It's fine. We're fine. (VIOLET *hides her face in* AGNES's *skirt.*) Malcolm's out with his mates playing footie. He knows to come home when he hears the siren.
ERNIE	You needn't worry, Luv.
AGNES	The bloody krauts almost hit the Five Lamps a couple of weeks ago. He knows they're getting close. That lad… he'll be the death of me.
ERNIE	The siren was just a practice call. I saw him. We had a wee kick-about. He's home now, in the yard, cleaning his boots before coming in.

AGNES	I have Mrs. Mussum looking after our Maureen and Timmy, so—
ERNIE	I don't like them over there.
AGNES	I had no choice, did I? I needed to be with our Violet.
ERNIE	I'll fetch them in a minute.
AGNES	How was your day, then?
ERNIE	Same. Although I do have a bit of news, if you can call it that.
AGNES	Oh yeah?
ERNIE	Our Malcolm just told me that Peter signed up for the R.A.F.
AGNES	Peter Mussum?
ERNIE	His Mam's been crying all day, he says.
AGNES	She should of said! Oh, we need get our Timmy and Maureen back home. She won't be—
ERNIE	A few more minutes won't hurt. It'll be a good distraction for her.
AGNES	I suspect Peter felt he'd be safer fighting the war in the skies, than home with the end of his father's belt.
ERNIE	Let's hope he'll be working on the expansion of the air field than fighting in the skies. No father in his right mind, who lived the horrors of the first war, would be allowing their son to join.
VIOLET	(*Mumbles.*) You won't let our Malcolm—
ERNIE	He's only 14, Luv. The war won't last long enough for him to join. Churchill's got the spitfires defending the Channel. Those lads... and now Peter, won't let us down.
AGNES	Joining any war, at any age, will be over my dead body. I won't have any child of mine—

ERNIE (*To* AGNES.) How did it go, then?

VIOLET (*Mumbles.*) I'm going to die a lonely, gummy spinster! (*Hides her face in* AGNES *skirt.*)

AGNES (*To* ERNIE.) It went fine, Luv. They were able to drain all the poison. They had to remove a fair bit of her gums, but they said they can build them back out so new teeth will fit. She just needs time to heal.

ERNIE (*Empathetically looking at* VIOLET.) They were good to let you take time off from your job at the Erimus, eh, Luv? I bet they're missing you in that kitchen today.

AGNES Our Gladys has done her best to keep her job open, but Violet will need more time to heal than what they're prepared to give.

ERNIE Is there 'owt else your sister can do?

AGNES I suspect they're already looking for a replacement.

VIOLET (*Mumbles.*) Oh no!

ERNIE Their loss. (*To* VIOLET.) Don't you worry, Luv, there'll be lots of hotels around who are hiring.

AGNES (*To* ERNIE.) Not since the war started, Luv. Our Gladys says they'll have lots of young lasses to choose from and probably pay them less than they did our Violet.

ERNIE Well, I didn't like her working there anyway. Goodness only knows what goes on. I've heard the rumours.

AGNES My sister was very good... kept a keen eye on our Violet. Made sure she was always... you know, safe.

ERNIE Well, as much as the extra wages helped, they can find a new scullery maid. (*Strokes* VIOLET's *hair.*) Our Violet's care comes first.

VIOLET (*Mumbles.*) Oh dad!

ERNIE — (*To* VIOLET.) I was thinking about you all day, Luv. Worried sick, I was.

AGNES — (*Stands.*) I was just going to put kettle on.

ERNIE — I'll put it on. You sit yourself down.

AGNES — You've been on your feet all day, Luv, I can—

ERNIE — You've had a full day yourself, Pet.

VIOLET — I wish the poison had killed me! Ow! (*Comforts her mouth.*)

ERNIE — (*To* VIOLET.) Time's the great healer, Violet, Luv.

VIOLET — (*Mumbles.*) If you say so.

ERNIE — We all get over life's setbacks… in time.

AGNES — (*Remembering* RODNEY.) Some worse than losing *teeth*.

ERNIE — I were 25 when I had all me teeth out. Mind you, I didn't have many good ones left. Most were rotting. You need lots of money to keep your own teeth. Well, healthy ones.

AGNES — I was 23, soon after you were born. (VIOLET *looks up at her Mam.*)

ERNIE — (*Kisses* AGNES *on the cheek.*) I knew your Mam with her own teeth back in the day, and with the ones she has now. And I can tell you, I love her more each passing day and her teeth have nowt to do with it.

AGNES — (*Blushes and kisses* ERNIE.) You're a good man, Ernie Ogden.

ERNIE — And you, Agnes Ogden, are the love of my life.

VIOLET — (*Mumbles.*) You'd already fallen in love before you were toothless. (*Runs out of room.*) Nobody will ever want to marry me! (EXIT.)

(TRANSITION)

SEPTEMBER 1943

EXTERIOR OF HEAD WRIGHTSON & CO, A MUNITIONS FACTORY IN THORNABY

(LETTIE *and* VIOLET *are having a smoke outside against the back door of the building.*)

VIOLET	(*Laughing*.) Well I had to leave, didn't I? Me-Mam had another baby—
LETTIE	Eeee, still going at it – at her age – with a war on. (*Chuckles*.)
VIOLET	She's not *that* old, Lettie. (*Chuckles*.) When our Dennis was born I said to meself, *Vi, you'll not be sticking 'round to help raise this one. Get out while you can.* I don't want to be one of those spinsters that never experiences life.
LETTIE	You did right, Luv.
VIOLET	I enjoy living with me-Auntie Gladdy at the Queen's Hotel. She lets me tinkle on the piano any time I want. She's says the guests enjoy me playing.
LETTIE	I wish I had family close by so I could get out. Me-Dad still has me under a curfew, for crissakes. Says, *a lass out past ten is only asking for trouble.*
VIOLET	But I was happy to leave me job at the Queens. Working *and* living with me Aunty was not... well, let's say, it was ruining our relationship – a bit smothering.
LETTIE	I don't know how she does it? You know, managing without a man.
VIOLET	She's manager at The Queen's. I guess it pays well.
LETTIE	You need a bloke for more than just money.
VIOLET	When the jobs were posted for here, I thought, they must be desperate with all the lads fighting abroad, they might even take me on. (*Laugh.*)

LETTIE	Don't talk daft! You're one of the best bomb welders in all of Wrightson's!
VIOLET	Me-Mam hates wars – I mean *really* hates them. I just used to think war were silly, but... it's created a job for me, so I guess—
LETTIE	You can thank Hitler.
VIOLET	(*Laugh.*) But he won't be thanking us for our bombs, will he? (*They laugh.*)
LETTIE	Coming to the dance Saturday?
VIOLET	Nah, me-Mam likes me to visit when I can. Gives her a break from the youngens.
LETTIE	You just said—
VIOLET	(*Laughing.*) I know! I know!
LETTIE	Shall we start calling you *spinster* now? Or, wait! Are you one of them... you know, that play for the *other* team?
VIOLET	Lettie? No! Of course not!
LETTIE	Well, you need to come out with the gang more. Get some experience under your belt.
VIOLET	Truth be told, our Maureen's old enough to help out with wee Timmy and Dennis – it's bath night – so... I go mostly for a visit. We chat about... lots of things. We're quite close.
LETTIE	My parents share nowt with me. Still think I'm too young to know about the ways of the world. I'm welding bloody bombs for heaven sakes! (*Laughs.*) How much more adult do I need to be?
VIOLET	Before I joined Wrightson's, I'd only done cleaning jobs. A munitions factory was a *proper* job. So, me-Mam said, *we need to talk*. I thought she were going to tell me about... you know... blokes an' stuff.

Blooming Violet

LETTIE	Me-Mam told me nowt about *that* stuff. *Cooking and cleaning – that's all I needed to know*, she'd say. I learned most stuff, stuff we *should* be told, from me cousin Deborah. She'd been around the block a few times, so she says.
VIOLET	It were bigger than that, Lettie.
LETTIE	Nowt is bigger than knowing about the birds and bees, Vi, Luv. (*Pause. Waiting.*) Well, go on, then, spit it out!
VIOLET	So, me-Mam tells me that me-Dad – Ernie Ogden – isn't really me-Dad.
LETTIE	Bloody hell! That's a bit of a bombshell.
VIOLET	She were married before, you see, to a soldier named Rodney Macdonald. Me-Mam said he were the love of her life, back then. But he died when I were only six weeks old.
LETTIE	Geezus, Vi, Luv!
VIOLET	I never really questioned why me last name was Macdonald, and everyone else in the family were Ogden.
LETTIE	Did you think you were adopted?
VIOLET	No – nothing like that. I just thought I was an Ogden with a different last name. (*Laughs.*) Doesn't really make sense, does it?
LETTIE	Does your brothers and sister know?
VIOLET	Me-Mam said nobody asked and nobody need know – none of their bloody business. Well, I guess it was *my* business.
LETTIE	You can say that again! Knowing who your real father was is very much *your* business! It's not like you were a bastard, conceived out of wedlock or... the result of a sordid affair with a married man, right?
VIOLET	Crickey, Lettie, nothing like *that*! They were married! Just not for a long time. I think she were afraid it would change me feelings for me-Dad – Ernie. But, as far as I'm concerned, he *is* me-Dad. Always has, and always will be.

LETTIE	Me cousin Martha, on me-Mam's side, has a different dad. Well, we suspect. She's the youngest of seven. Nobody says nowt but, in a family of brunettes, she's the only blonde!
VIOLET	I'm a ginger in a family of brunette's. (*Laughs.*) I guess he were a red-head.
LETTIE	I love your hair!
VIOLET	Me-Mam swears I got me talent for singing and piano playing from him, too. She can't carry a tune. (*Chuckles.*) She said, *he were a lovely singer*, being Scottish, and all.
LETTIE	Ohhh, maybe you're related to Robert the Bruce.
VIOLET	Well, if I am, I didn't get the bloody brave gene! (*They both laugh.*)
LETTIE	So why tell you at all?
VIOLET	Me birth certificate states that me father is this Rodney Macdonald bloke. I'd never seen nor needed it before. But me-Mam said that when I was applying at Wrightson's, they'd be asking for identification. So, best to let me in on the family *secret* before I make a right berk of meself. (*Chuckles.*)
LETTIE	I wonder who else knew? I mean, I couldn't keep a secret like that!
VIOLET	*You* can't keep the colour of your knickers to yourself. (*Chuckles.*)
LETTIE	Beige again today. (*They both laugh.*)
VIOLET	Then went on to tell me about the time when I had me teeth out and had to buy new ones.
LETTIE	How old were you? I were only 15.
VIOLET	(*Shocked.*) You too? I was almost 17. Anyway, I had wondered where she'd got the money, but she never said. Money was really tight back then, you see.

LETTIE	Oh, I remember. I never wore a pair of shoes of me own until last year! No wonder me feet are all scrunched and me toes are crooked.
VIOLET	A few months back, though, she explained. She still had her wedding ring from Rodney, you see, and a couple of other pieces of jewelry he'd given her from when he were in India.
LETTIE	India… that's pretty exotic. Rodney the Bruce - in India. (*Laughs at her own joke.*)
VIOLET	She sold the ring and all his jewelry gifts to the pawnbrokers so I could have new teeth.
LETTIE	Goldmeyers? On the High Street?
VIOLET	I don't know.
LETTIE	Most likely. They're known for taking advantage of folk when they're desperate. They probably paid only a quarter of what they were worth. Shysters, the lot of them!
VIOLET	I told her she were silly to sell them, but she said that Rodney would have wanted them to help out his Violet.
LETTIE	It must have been hard for her, though, to sell her only memories of him – being the *love of her life*, an' all.
VIOLET	I think that's why she loves having me around, because… I'm all she has left from their short time together.
LETTIE	What a beautiful love story. (*Sighs.*) Your poor dad.
VIOLET	Which one?
LETTIE	Ernie! When you think about it, it's sad. He married a woman who were in love with another man.
VIOLET	Like 'eckers, *poor* Ernie. Apparently he'd loved me-Mam for *years* and was sad only when she went off and married this Rodney bloke. Mam said that me-Dad, Ernie, were grateful for the second chance.

LETTIE	Well, she must have fallen in love with him at some point! I mean...they must've made it work... she had your brothers and sister with him. (*Laughing*.)
VIOLET	I guess he did win her over. I've only ever known them to love each other. (*Big drag on her cigarette, dreamily*.) I hope I can find that depth of love... you know... with a bloke.

SFX – SOUND OF JEEP GOES BY AND MEN WHISTLING

LETTIE	(To *jeep*.) In your dreams, lover boy! (*To* VIOLET.) I think Percy's going to be at the dance.
VIOLET	Oh, ya! So he's finally asked you out then?
LETTIE	No – but I think he might on Saturday.
VIOLET	You'll already be there.
LETTIE	(*Laughing*.) For the following weekend, you silly-git. Maybe go to the pictures. *The Life and Death of Colonel Blimp* is playing at the Globe.
VIOLET	Another war movie – as if we need to see pictures of war when we're living it.
LETTIE	Yes, but this one has Roger Livesey in it... (*Swoons*.) and the gorgeous Deborah Kerr. Come with us.
VIOLET	Percy hasn't asked *you* yet. (*Chuckles*.) And I'm not going to be a pathetic gooseberry when you go out with him.
LETTIE	When he asks me, I'll tell him to bring a friend – for you.
VIOLET	I'm not *that* pathetic either. I can find me own blokes... when I'm ready.
LETTIE	You don't want to become a spinster like your Aunty Gladdy do you? Come with us on Saturday.
VIOLET	She seems happy enough without a bloke. And besides, I'm not even twenty yet – hardly a spinster. I have plenty of time—

LETTIE	We're in our prime now, Vi, Luv, we can't hold off too much longer.
VIOLET	Well, I'll hold off this weekend while you concentrate on Percy.
LETTIE	(*Pleading.*) Come on!
VIOLET	We're celebrating our Maureen's 12th birthday on Saturday.
LETTIE	Well, if you're sure.
VIOLET	I am. But you're a good friend to think of me.
LETTIE	The best, forever and a day.

(TRANSITION.)

May 8, 1945

THE HAREWOOD ARMS PUB, THORNABY

(LETTIE *sits in the snug with her face buried in her hands.*)

SFX – LOUD PUB CHATTER.

(ENTER VIOLET *holding a Union Jack flag. She looks around for* LETTIE.)

VIOLET	There you are! I've been looking all over the place for you. Why weren't you at work?
LETTIE	I… I…
VIOLET	Shift over, Luv. (*Sits down and lights a cigarette.*) Nobody got any work done anyway. They announced over the big speaker that Hitler surrendered! Isn't it wonderful? War has finally ended, Lettie. About bloody time, too. Streets are chock-a-block with people waving flags. (*Shouts.*) Open your curtains, Thornaby, and let your lights shine bright! No more air raids, no more rations… I haven't seen this much joy and happiness… (*Notices* LETTIE.) Lettie, Luv, you alright?
LETTIE	It's Percy.
VIOLET	Ohhh, what's he gone 'n' done now?
LETTIE	Gone and got himself killed, hasn't he!
VIOLET	Eeee, Lettie – what happened?
LETTIE	(*Hands a crumpled telegram to* VIOLET.) Our Percy's Mam brought it to the house this morning.
VIOLET	(*Reads telegram.*) I regret to inform you that your son, Private Percival Bottomley has succumbed to his injuries. STOP. He died May 1, 1945. STOP. His body will be repatriated for burial on May 10. STOP. (*Puts her arm around* LETTIE.) Oh, Lettie, Luv. I'm so sorry.
LETTIE	Eight days before the war ends - eight bloody days. Why couldn't he just keep his head down for eight more days?

VIOLET	He wouldn't have known it were going to end, would he? None of us did. We just hoped—
LETTIE	He were only 22, barely started his life.
VIOLET	His poor Mam and Dad – losing a son. Our Malcolm joined just a few months back. Me-Mam *and* Dad went ballistic! Lucky lad, though, hasn't been shipped overseas – stationed in Scotland as a guard at a P.O.W. camp.
LETTIE	(*Looking up at* VIOLET.) We were going to be married.
VIOLET	You never said!
LETTIE	Not officially.
VIOLET	Lettie Bottomley. (*Stifles a laugh.*)
LETTIE	We talked about it. Percy said we should wait 'til the war was over – so as to not tie me down.
VIOLET	It's not tying you down when you *want* to marry. You would have waited for him.
LETTIE	He said he wanted me to be free... you know... in case I met someone else. (*Breaks down.*)
VIOLET	That were considerate.
LETTIE	I'll never find another one like him.
VIOLET	Stupid war. Killing off our youngest and... best... and for what?
LETTIE	Oh, Vi, I'm crushed. I don't think I'll ever get over this.
VIOLET	You will, Luv. As me-Dad says, time's the great healer. But life won't be the same, will it? Living amongst all the rubble and destruction – families left without fathers – Mams losing their sons. (*Realization.*) There may not even be enough good lads left for *us* to marry.
LETTIE	Don't say that!

VIOLET   Well, it's true. We'll be spinsters together. (*They look at each other.*) I think we could do with a drink.

LETTIE   Thanks, Luv. Rum and Coca Cola.

VIOLET   Right. (*Goes to bar.*) Rum and Coca Cola for our Lettie, and one for me. She just found out her Percy was killed in the war. (*Comes back with two drinks.*) Cal didn't charge me. Said they were on the house – for Percy.

LETTIE   (*Raises her glass to the bar.*) Thank you.

VIOLET   Drinks should be free for everyone today.

LETTIE   Oh, Cal won't be that generous. His missus has a tight hold on the till.

VIOLET   (*Holds up her glass.*) To Percy.

LETTIE   (*Holds up her glass.*) To my Percy. I'll never forget you. (*They both drink.*)

VIOLET   Do you still have his letters?

LETTIE   Every one of them.

VIOLET   Well, that's summat to remember him by.

LETTIE   His writing was terrible but his words were beautiful.

VIOLET   You were lucky.

LETTIE   Lucky? I don't feel bloody lucky today.

VIOLET   You found love.

LETTIE   I don't recommend it, because it hurts like mad, right now.

VIOLET   For months you loved and were loved. That's more than I can say.

LETTIE   I was going to have him introduce his brother to you.

VIOLET   He has a brother? You never said. Keeping things close to the chest these days, aren't you?

LETTIE	I've always been a woman of discretion.
VIOLET	(*Sarcastic.*) Right. (*Interested.*) So, this brother—
LETTIE	I think he's a few years younger than Percy.
VIOLET	Then I'm too old, aren't I?
LETTIE	Ya never! Percy was… I knew as soon as I'd set eyes on him, he were the one for me.
VIOLET	You knew right away? But you were always falling out with him.
LETTIE	I was training him to be how I wanted him to be, wasn't I? And we were almost there. I used to dream about how our children would look, you know, Percy's and mine.
VIOLET	I don't know if I want children. I've practically raised me brothers and sister. I think I'm all mothered out!
LETTIE	Percy wanted a houseful. That's what he said.
VIOLET	He can say all he wants, but it wasn't him going to be having them though, was it? I've seen how they're born, with me-Mam, and let me tell you—
LETTIE	(*Breaks down.*) We won't be having any now!
VIOLET	(*Puts arm around* LETTIE.) Oh, Lettie, Luv – let it out. I think a little Vera would be the ticket right now. (*Sings a capella.*)

We'll meet again, Don't know where, don't know when
But I know we'll meet again some sunny day
Keep smiling through, Just like you always do
'Til the blue skies drive the dark clouds far away

(LETTIE *joins in.*) *So will you please say "Hello" to the folks that I know, Tell them I won't be long*
They'll be happy to know that as you saw me go
I was singing this song. We'll meet again
Don't know where, don't know when
But I know we'll meet again some sunny day.

INTERMISSION

ACT TWO

NOVEMBER 1949

SERGEANT'S MESS HALL IN STOCKTON

(LETTIE *and* VIOLET *in their Army Sergeant's uniform sit at a table having a drink.* KEN CLARKE *and* KEN LESTER *both in civilian clothing stand together on the other side of the room holding a pint each and smoking cigarettes.*)

    SFX – PIANO DANCE HALL MUSIC

VIOLET	Slim pickins tonight.
LETTIE	There's a few moseying about. (*Lights cigarette.*)
VIOLET	How's a lass supposed to find a mate when even a Sergeant's mess hall with their cheap ale can't draw the blokes out.
LETTIE	Lots got married as soon as the war ended, didn't they? No need to be out on the prowl anymore.
VIOLET	I waited too long. Me window of opportunity has closed. Blokes want younger lasses.
LETTIE	I'm so glad I found Tom when I did. You still good to be me Maid of Honour?
VIOLET	Eeee, I would have disowned you had you not asked.
LETTIE	I'm thinking February.
VIOLET	That's the same month our Malcolm got married.
LETTIE	You were a bridesmaid. I remember having to take in the bust-line on the dress Doreen made you wear. (*Chuckles.*)
VIOLET	You would remember *that*! (*Chuckles.*) Three years ago, now. Just out of the army, our Malcolm was – goes to visit his Doreen and the next thing you know she's… in the family way.

LETTIE	It happens. It must have been her hormones to choose that sickly yellow. (*Chuckles.*)
VIOLET	It wasn't so bad. It couldn't be too bright, could it – being a winter wedding an' all? They're expecting baby number two in a couple of weeks.
LETTIE	I'm thinking dark blue for my bridesmaids.
VIOLET	(*Concerned.*) Is that why the short engagement? You and Tom—
LETTIE	Preggers? Giv'over. I'm not daft!
VIOLET	Just like a bloke, though. Back from front lines to the home front and it's: *Hello Doreen, Luv. It's been a while. Let's have a cuddle...* and poof... up the duff she goes. (*They both laugh.*)
LETTIE	Tom and I don't *have* to wed. But it was touch-and-go a couple of months back.
VIOLET	You mean... so... you... you and Tom have... already... you know?
LETTIE	Of course! But only recently. I wanted to give him a test drive, you know, before I really committed.
VIOLET	You and Tom... you never said!
LETTIE	Me-Mam wants me to get married in the same church as her and me-Dad.
VIOLET	Will you still wear *white*, then? I mean... since it'll be in a church and all?
LETTIE	Of course! We only go at Christmas and Easter – so the vicar doesn't really know me. But I'm having the reception here. A good old knees-up.
VIOLET	In the mess hall?

LETTIE	With Tom and I being Sergeants, we can. And it's free! Well, not the drinks, mind. And me-Mam will make the sausage rolls, sarnies and cakes. I've already asked our Sergeant-Major.
VIOLET	They only promoted us to sergeant because they like us singing at the Saturday dances.
LETTIE	Good a reason as any.

SFX – VOICE OVER: "COME ON GIRLS, LET'S 'AVE YOU UP HERE. PUT YOUR HANDS TOGETHER. LET'S HERE IT FOR LETTIE, EDNA AND VI."

LETTIE	(*Shouts back.*) No Edna tonight, Luv. (*To* VIOLET.) She had to go away for a wee while, didn't she?
VIOLET	She never said.
LETTIE	Well, she wouldn't, would she? Nobody's supposed to know. But I found out.
VIOLET	Where'd she go?
LETTIE	London. I think she'll be gone for a… few months. (*Winks.*)
VIOLET	A few months?
LETTIE	Until… you know… until it's… over.
VIOLET	(*Shocked.*) She's preg—
LETTIE	Shhhh! Come on, let's get up.
VIOLET	(*Panic.*) I've only had one drink, I'm not ready. I need at least two more.
LETTIE	(*Shouts out.*) We'll do Andrew Sisters.
VIOLET	(*Panicking. Gulps down the remainder of her drink.*) Without Edna?
LETTIE	We can do it. (*Stands. Shouts out.*) *Don't Sit Under The Apple Tree.*

VIOLET	(*Stands. Looking out.*) Alright – there's not many here anyway. (*See's the two KEN'S.*) Hang-on, who's that?
LETTIE	(*Shielding her eyes to see.*) Where? (*They both make their way to the stage.*)
VIOLET	(*Points.*) There.
LETTIE	Oh, that's Ken. A friend of our Tom's.
VIOLET	(*Smiles.*) Hmmm.
LETTIE	(*Surprised.*) Did we find a needle in the haystack? A bloke that has actually caught the eye of the elusive Violet Macdonald?
VIOLET	Just inquiring.

SFX- PIANO MUSIC "DON'T SIT UNDER THE APPLE TREE"

VIOLET/LETTIE	*Don't sit under the apple tree with anyone else but me* *Anyone else but me, anyone else but me* *No! No! No!* *Just remember that I've been true to nobody else but you* *So just be true to me* *Don't go walking down lovers' lane with anyone else but me* *Anyone else but me, anyone else but me* *No! No! No!* *Don't start showing off all your charms in somebody else's arms* *You must be true to me* *I'm so afraid that the plans we made underneath those moonlit skies* *Will fade away and you're bound to stray if the stars get in your eyes* *So, don't sit under the apple tree with anyone else but me* *You're my L-O-V-E.*
VIOLET	(*Puts up her hand.*) That's enough for now. We'll do more later.

SFX - MUSIC STOPS. APPLAUSE.

LETTIE	What's up, Vi? Not feeling well.
VIOLET	No, I just…
LETTIE	You upset about Edna, because she—
VIOLET	No, well, yes… but… I mean…
LETTIE	(*Follows* VIOLET's *gaze*.) Oh, I see. You haven't taken your eyes off him.
VIOLET	Was I that obvious?
LETTIE	I'm surprised a hole didn't burrow its way through his head. Want to meet him?
VIOLET	I wasn't staring at him the *whole* time.
LETTIE	(*Grabs* VIOLET's *hand but* VIOLET *resists*.) Come on, I'll introduce you. I've met him a couple of times. He's a nice bloke… for a bloke.
VIOLET	Maybe I should powder me nose first.
LETTIE	You're beautiful enough. You're prettier than lazy-eyed Edna and someone found her attractive enough for a roll in the hay… uggghh… let's not go there! I want you to strike while your iron's hot.

    SFX – DANCE MUSIC IN BACKGROUND

(LETTIE *drags* VIOLET *over to where* KEN CLARKE *and* KEN LESTER *stand. The lads stub-out their cigarettes on seeing the girls wander over.*)

LETTIE	(*To* KEN LESTER.) Hi Ken.
KEN LESTER	Hello, Luv.
LETTIE	I want to introduce you to my friend, Vi. She's going to be me Maid of Honour at mine and Tom's wedding.
KEN LESTER	Right. Hello, Luv.
VIOLET	Hello. (*To* LETTIE.) A word! (*Pulls* LETTIE *to the side. Loud whisper*.) Not him! The other one!

LETTIE	The other... Crikey! I don't know who the other one is.
KEN LESTER	Is there a problem?
LETTIE	No... no... I just... who's your friend?
KEN LESTER	Ahh – well... he happens to be a Ken too. Ken Clarke.
LETTIE	A pair of Ken's. (*Starts laughing.*) Hear that Vi? A pair of Ken's. (*To* KEN CLARKE.) I'm Lettie, she's Violet.
VIOLET	Just Vi.
KEN	(*To* VIOLET.) Hello, *just* Vi.
VIOLET	(*To* KEN.) Hiya.

(*There is an awkward pause.*)

KEN LESTER	Ahhh... Ken here's just back from a stint in Palestine.
LETTIE	Weren't you there too, with our Tom?
KEN LESTER	We were – but I returned a few months ago. Ken and I go way back – school days.
KEN	He's why I didn't leave Stockton after passing my 11 Plus. I just couldn't trust this eegit to stay out of trouble. (*Chuckles.*)
LETTIE	You passed your 11 Plus? What in hells-bells are you doing here?
KEN	You have to have money to move to where them Grammar schools are. I'm the eldest of four boys – barely enough money to keep four young lads fed, let alone educated.
LETTIE	I don't know anyone who passed their 11 plus. I'm impressed.
KEN LESTER	Hey, aren't you engaged to Tom?
LETTIE	Jealous?
KEN LESTER	Where is Tom?

LETTIE	Probably in some back alley, seeing a man, who knows a man, who knows a man, to get some cheap cigs. Anything to avoid the dance floor.
KEN LESTER	Sheila's in the loo. I think the smoke's getting to her.
LETTIE	(*To* KEN LESTER.) Oh, so it's working out with you two, then. Tom never said.
KEN LESTER	Getting hitched later this month. That's why Ken here is back home. Best man an' all.
LETTIE	Crikey, you've only just met her.
KEN LESTER	Let's just say, we *need* to hurry things along.
KEN	See? Trouble! (*Chuckles*.) Not back in time.
LETTIE	Ohhhh! I *do* see. (*Whispers to* VIOLET.) Just like your Malcolm… *and* Edna. (*Blurts out*.) She's got a bun in the oven.
KEN LESTER	(*To* VIOLET.) You too? Wait 'til I tell Sheila.
KEN	Oh!
LETTIE	Not Vi! (*Laughs*.) Eeeee, no! She's not even been—
VIOLET	Lettie! Shhhh!
LETTIE	(*To* KEN.) Anyway, that'll be why the smoke's getting to her.
VIOLET	Poor Sheila.
KEN	I don't know about that! Ken here's a pretty good catch, I would say – a Sergeant with good prospects.
KEN LESTER	Ta, mate!
LETTIE	Good for Sheila, is what I say. Best to get on with things in case another war breaks out.
KEN	Better bloody not! I won't be sticking around if it does.
LETTIE	Gunning for a better life, then, Ken? Hear that, Vi?

KEN	There's more to life than living out your days in a small town in the northeast... like being in a goldfish bowl.
KEN LESTER	(*Looks around.*) We were going to get married anyway. We're in love. There she is... my little bread pudding. Cheerio. (EXIT.)
LETTIE	(*Looks at* VIOLET *and* KEN *looking at each other.*) Well... I'll see if I can find our Tom.
VIOLET	Tom?
LETTIE	Yeah, you know, that bloke I'm marrying? (To VIOLET *on the side.*) Eeee, you've got it bad, Luv. (*Chuckles.*)
KEN	Who me, or her? (*Embarrassed* VIOLET *chuckles.*)
LETTIE	Watch yourself with these smart blokes, Vi, Luv. (*Walks away, but keeps looking back to check on* VIOLET. EXIT.)
VIOLET	(*To* LETTIE.) Ta-rah! (*To* KEN.) So, not keen on Stockton?
KEN	Born and bred, but... there's a more... exciting world outside of England that really appeals to me.
VIOLET	I've never travelled... well, apart from a day trip to the seaside.
KEN	You work in the kitchen here, don't you? I saw you yesterday.
VIOLET	Uh, huh. Once war ended I joined the W.A.C.s. I had a fair bit of experience so they put me in the kitchen. But before that, I worked at Head Wrightson's – during the war.
KEN	Munitions factory! What did you do there?
VIOLET	I welded bombs.
KEN	(*Impressed.*) I got to witness the result of your work.
VIOLET	Have you eaten here?

KEN	No, I'm not stationed in the U.K. much. I'm an M.P. – Military Police.
VIOLET	I know what an M.P. is. (*Chuckles*.)
KEN	And, you know how to build bombs.
VIOLET	That I do. Well, I weld them together.
KEN	I've just returned from Palestine.
VIOLET	Ya, your friend said. What was it like there?
KEN	An eye opener, to be honest. Dry, dusty – a lot of issues between the Arabs and the Israelis. I suspect the conflict there will be a long one.
VIOLET	How long were you there?
KEN	Let's see, I was in Palestine from '46 to just a few days ago. I was in Germany before that.
VIOLET	(*Impressed*.) With Hitler?
KEN	No, he did himself in before I got there.
VIOLET	Coward!
KEN	He was! I joined up in '45, a week before the war ended, actually.
VIOLET	I waited 'til the war were over too. Me-Mam would never have forgiven me for joining up with a war on.
KEN	I couldn't wait – the silly eegit I was. Me-Mam just had wee Ted a year earlier. It got pretty tight with me, two younger brothers and a wailing baby in our three-bedroom terrace house.
VIOLET	Why did you wait? You know… why not join earlier – to fight in the war?

KEN	I wasn't old enough, was I? I was only 17 – I wouldn't be 18 until that October – so I lied and said I couldn't find my birth certificate. They didn't care. Needed to replenish the troops, I imagine.
VIOLET	(*Thoughtful.*) Probably replacing Percy.
KEN	Who?
VIOLET	Never mind. (*Suddenly.*) How old are you now, then?
KEN	22. You?
VIOLET	(*She's taken aback.*) What… umm… were you doing in the mess hall if you weren't eating here? You know, when you said you saw me?
KEN	Well I must say you run the kitchen like a proper drill Sergeant. (*Chuckles.*)
VIOLET	I have to! Lots of mouths to feed in a short amount of time – and with many surfaces to clean – not to mention limited rations, it's always a challenge.
KEN	I was on K.P. duty because—
VIOLET	I don't remember seeing you. And I think I would remember—
KEN	Well, I was keeping my head down, wasn't I? Potato peeler in one hand and my pride in the other. (*Chuckles.*)
VIOLET	What did you do wrong? You've only just got back? (*Chuckles.*)
KEN	I… took apart one of the officer's jeeps.
VIOLET	Was it on the fritz?
KEN	That was the issue, you see. It ran beautifully. That's *why* I took it apart. So I could learn how to put it back together again.
VIOLET	(*Laughing.*) You want to build jeeps?

KEN	Once I learned how to build an engine, I knew I could build any automobile. I love to build things. And it's the best way for me to learn.
VIOLET	I thought they had those kinds of things, you know, learning things, in books for you bright lads.
KEN	I read those too! But you learn even better hands-on.
LETTIE	(ENTER. *Holds 3 drinks*.) Tom bought us drinks. Here you go. (*Puts them on table.*)
VIOLET	(*Stands and grabs* LETTIE *away and whispers loud in her ear.*) He's only 22!
LETTIE	Crikey, he doesn't look like a bairn.
VIOLET	(*Loud whisper.*) I'm 26! I'm too old for him.
LETTIE	(*Loud whisper.*) *He* obviously doesn't think so.
VIOLET	(*Loud whisper.*) Shhhh! The lighting is dim in here – he can't see me properly.
LETTIE	(*Loud whisper.*) Then don't tell him your age.
VIOLET	(*Loud whisper.*) He already asked.
LETTIE	(*Loud whisper.*) Did you tell him?
VIOLET	(*Loud whisper.*) No! Of course not… but… oh what's the use – might as well stop it before it gets started.
LETTIE	(*To* KEN.) What's your view on older women?
VIOLET	Lettie!
KEN	(*Taken back.*) How… you mean like me Mam or Gran?
LETTIE	No… like—
VIOLET	I'm 26.
LETTIE	(*Justifying.*) She *just* turned 26, a couple of weeks ago.

KEN	Right. Well if we're *fessing* up about stuff, I should let you know... I'm not a Sergeant. I'm only a Private.
LETTIE	I thought you 11-Plus folks were all officers. How'd you get in?

SFX – DANCE MUSIC SWELLS UP

KEN	Ken's the Sarge. I'm here as his guest.
LETTIE	There you go, Vi, Luv – more concerned with his lack of rank than your age. Ooo, I luv this song. Gotta get our Tom on the dance floor. (EXITS.)
KEN	(*To* VIOLET.) Want to dance?
VIOLET	(*Chuckles.*) If you're okay dancing with an older woman.
KEN	Are you okay dancing with just a Private?
VIOLET	Rankings are overrated. I'm a Sarge only because I can sing. (*Stands.*)
KEN	I'm a Private because I can't. (*They both laugh. Takes her hand and twirls her around.*) You're pretty light on your feet, too.
VIOLET	Me-Mam was a dancer, when she were young.
KEN	Well she passed that gene on... a lass who can sing *and* dance!
VIOLET	*And* weld a bomb!
KEN	That's an eleven-plus in my book. (*Twirls her around again and then brings her in close.*)

(TRANSITION)

July, 1950

THE PIER AT REDCAR

SFX – SOUNDS OF WAVES AND SEAGULLS IN BACKGROUND.

SFX – SOUND OF A MOTORCYCLE APPROACHING AND THEN THE ENGINE SHUTS OFF.

(VIOLET *with a scarf on her head and* KEN *taking off his bike gloves.* ENTER.)

VIOLET (*Laughing.*) I've never ridden on a bike before.

KEN Never?

VIOLET I mean a motorbike.

KEN Fun, aren't they?

VIOLET I wouldn't exactly call it *fun*. I had to hold on to you for dear life the whole way. (*Takes off her headscarf and fixes her hair.*)

KEN That's why I wanted to take you for a ride.

VIOLET (*Playful.*) Giv'over! Motorbikes cost a bit of dosh. They must pay you well at Hills.

KEN That job will do for now – and it's better than the army, that's for sure.

VIOLET You have your sights on a different career, then?

KEN Different career – different life all together.

VIOLET It's good to have drive, I guess… you know… for better things.

KEN My bike is a good start to get my *drive* going. (*Chuckles.*) What about you?

VIOLET Me?

KEN Yes, you! What is that you want out of life, Vi?

VIOLET: I'm not sure. I know there should be more to it than... where I am right now.

KEN: Are you ready for something different?

VIOLET: Yes... and no. (*Chuckles.*) I mean... I enjoyed me time in the W.A.C.s, but once Lettie and Edna left... well... and then when me Aunty Gladdy got me my supervisor position back at the Queens... well, I don't know... I just feel like I'm going backwards. (*Awkward Chuckle.*) But there has to be more... right?

KEN: Life is what we make of it, Luv. A *good* life, a *satisfying* life, is filled with challenges, risks and adventure.

VIOLET: Like riding a motorbike for the first time? (*Chuckles.*)

KEN: It's a good start. I practically built it myself. I picked it up for a song.

VIOLET: Is this the same dodgy bike you drove over to the mess hall last spring?

KEN: It sure is. Remember? I took a photo of you.

VIOLET: I thought for sure it would fall apart as soon as I sat on it.

KEN: It was a mess when the bloke sold it to me.

VIOLET: Your jeep dismantling days are paying off! (*Chuckles.*)

KEN: Actually, I'm quite chuffed. This is my first run.

VIOLET: (*Playful.*) You used me as a human guinea pig?

KEN: Just provided you with risk and adventure – rolled into one. You're welcome. (*Chuckles.*)

VIOLET: Glad you didn't tell me *that* before we left Stockton. (*Chuckles. Takes a big breath looking out over the sea.*) I do love the seaside, though.

KEN: Me too. (*Stares out over sea. Pause. Rummages up courage.*) Vi?

VIOLET	Yes?
KEN	I'm happy you came with me today.
VIOLET	Of course! I enjoy… being with you, too.
KEN	Do you? Because I was wondering…
VIOLET	Yes?
KEN	Ken is married to Sheila and has started a family—
VIOLET	Started a family and *then* got married.
KEN	(*Chuckles.*) I guess the order does matter. And your Lettie and Tom are married.
VIOLET	She's expecting their first.
KEN	Oh, right. Tom never said.
VIOLET	She just found out herself. Not sure she's even told Tom yet – it's early days. (*Chuckles.*) Mind you, she can't keep anything to herself. Soon, she'll be blabbering to all an' sundry.
KEN	Tom will be well suited.
VIOLET	And Edna, she's getting married next month. Just a registry ceremony. They want to put any wedding money towards a house instead.
KEN	That's prudent. (*Pause.*) Are you *good* with a wedding… I mean, like that?
VIOLET	At a registry? I've never thought about it, to be honest. I guess when the time comes, *if* the time comes, I'll know better.
KEN	So not keen on getting married… right now?
VIOLET	(*Gets nervous as she is sees where this is going.*) Well… I'm not sure. I've just left the army and made supervisor at the Queen's Hotel—

KEN	You don't have to give up your job, like in the olden days… you know… if you get married.
VIOLET	I… I just… I feel like I'm treading water, and then… the next minute, what I really want to do is… break free.
KEN	Free? Like, move away? Travel?
VIOLET	(*Swinging around*.) I've only lived with me-Mam and Dad, and then with me Aunty Gladdy – never even been out of the northeast. The world scares me. I want the world to be me oyster, as they say, but I… I don't feel prepared.
KEN	(*Resigned*.) Seafood it is. Fancy fish and chips?
VIOLET	(*Relieved*.) I would never say no to fish and chips.
KEN	(*Gets up his nerve again*.) Would you ever say no… to *me*?
VIOLET	(*Apprehensive*.) That would depend on the question.
KEN	It's a pretty important question.
VIOLET	(*Big sigh*.) Ken, I think I know what's going on here.
KEN	(*Elusive*.) You do?
VIOLET	No Ken and Sheila—
KEN	Well, they have their hands full with the baby coming.
VIOLET	What about Edna and Jack – Lettie and Tom? Why aren't they here?
KEN	I asked Tom to keep everyone away. He said Lettie wasn't feeling well, anyway.
VIOLET	Oh, I must trundle over when we get back… see how's she's feeling.
KEN	This is our first time… on our own.
VIOLET	So it is.

KEN	You always seem to prefer friends around whenever we… well, when we go out. I ask you, just you, and the next thing I know… there's eight of us.
VIOLET	Don't you like our friends?
KEN	Yes, but today, I wanted to be with *just* you.
VIOLET	The fact is, Ken, I'm not… very experienced with… going out.
KEN	With lads?
VIOLET	I've never… I mean… you're the first bloke that—
KEN	(*Shocked*.) That you've gone out with?
VIOLET	Yes.
KEN	How can that be? You're lovely. And you're… well, 26!
VIOLET	(*Defensive*.) It's not that blokes weren't interested! I could've had me pick.
KEN	I believe that would be true!
VIOLET	It's just… I didn't… I was… well… oh, I don't know why. I just never… I'm not sure I want the responsibility, you know, that comes with… being married.
KEN	(*Defensive*.) Who said anything about marriage?
VIOLET	You did! Didn't you? Isn't this what… Listen, you're a very smart man, Ken Clarke. You can build things, you read books all the time, you know about all sorts of stuff, you can build motorbikes for goodness sakes…. you're adventurous and you're… you're very handsome.
KEN	(*Smiles*.) Well, except for the handsome part, what do the other things have to do with getting wed?
VIOLET	You deserve a lass who's as smart and as… as worldly as you.
KEN	Don't talk daft, Vi. You're smart.

VIOLET	Don't underestimate yourself.
KEN	I'm destined for bigger things, I know.
VIOLET	See that? Right there – confident and smart.
KEN	So are you Vi! You know the practicalities of life… and do them very well.
VIOLET	Like what?
KEN	There's more to you than just what you do as a job… I see it. I know it! I think together we would—
VIOLET	Well… I'm not… *experienced*… you know… in other ways… with lads.
KEN	So? Everyone starts out not knowing how… things go.
VIOLET	I bet *you* do, though, don't you?
KEN	A little – I guess. But that has nothing—
VIOLET	And that's how you gained… experience. Hands on!
KEN	Well, yah – but, mostly I learned from smutty magazines.
VIOLET	You read those?
KEN	(*Smirk*.) Not so much read… mostly studied the pictures.
VIOLET	(*Rolling her eyes*.) I don't know why I even bother.
KEN	(*Leaning in*.) Well you were bothered enough, or should I say *curious* enough to come here on your own, with me, on my bike for the first time, *luring* you to the seaside.
VIOLET	(*Coy*.) No, well…maybe. But—
KEN	(*Toying*.) And a promise of Redcar's famous fish 'n' chips.
VIOLET	(*Talking in code in reference to the somewhat proposal*.) I'm going to say *no* to fish 'n' chips, right now – but would say *yes* to an ice cream, instead – for now.

KEN	(*Dejected*.) If that's what you prefer.
VIOLET	It is. (*Pause*.) You're not mad, are you?
KEN	I'm disappointed, Luv. I can't hide that.
VIOLET	You could have your choice from lots of girls, Ken.
KEN	Maybe, but I'm not interested in other girls, Vi.
VIOLET	Why me?
KEN	(*Strokes a hair from her forehead. Gentle*.) You're lovely… talented… and you're fun. And you like riding my motorbike.
VIOLET	(*Smiles*.) Well, I think *like* is a bit strong of a word.
KEN	Ready for another spin then?
VIOLET	Not yet! I haven't recovered from getting here.
KEN	(*Leans in*.) I'll wait, Violet Macdonald, as long as need be.
VIOLET	(*Hopeful*.) Really?
KEN	As long as you need.
VIOLET	(*Looks him in the eye. She's just been won over*.) Maybe not as long as you think, Mr. Clarke. You can put your arm around me now, if you like.
KEN	I *would* like that – a lot! (*And he does*.)
(TRANSITION)	

FEBRUARY 24, 1951

TWO SEPARATE READY-ROOMS AT ST. PAUL'S CHURCH, STOCKTON-ON-TEES

KEN LESTER *and* KEN *are in one spotlight.* VIOLET *and* LETTIE (*who is eight months pregnant*) *are in another spotlight. Each respectively getting ready for* KEN *and* VIOLET's *wedding.* KEN *is currently in a crisp white shirt and trousers with a jacket, tie and boutonniere to be added over the course of dialogue.* VIOLET *is in a house robe.* KEN LESTER *and* LETTIE *are already in their wedding attire as Maid of Honour and Best Man.*)

KEN	Got the ring?
KEN LESTER	Check. (*Helps* KEN *with tie.*)
KEN	Honeymoon suite booked?
KEN LESTER	Check.
KEN	What if she doesn't show up?
KEN LESTER	Of course she'll show up. Vi's not going to let you down. She said *yes*, so she'll be there.
KEN	It was a *hesitant* yes.
KEN LESTER	Sheila's loaned Vi her wedding dress, for crissakes. She'll be there.
KEN	Just being paranoid, right?
KEN LESTER	You are.
(TRANSITION.)	
VIOLET	I'm so nervous.
LETTIE	Every bride's nervous on her wedding day. (*Fussing with* VIOLET's *hair.*)
VIOLET	If we're nervous, it must mean... we're not sure.

Blooming Violet

LETTIE	No, it means we want everything to go to plan but we're too busy getting ourselves all gorgeous 'n' stuff, so we have to leave all the wedding details to others. At this stage of the game, it's all about trust, Luv.
VIOLET	I couldn't care less about any of that.
LETTIE	Then you have no reason to be nervous.
VIOLET	I'm nervous about what happens *after* the wedding.
LETTIE	That's all taken care of. Sheila's not here yet – but your Mam and Aunty Gladdy are with Maureen and Edna setting up the hall right now, and—
VIOLET	No! (*Turns her head to have* LETTIE's *large belly in her face.*) After *that*!
LETTIE	(*Chuckles.*) Oh!
(TRANSITION.)	
KEN	I think it's tonight she's hesitant about.
KEN LESTER	(*Helps* KEN *with his jacket.*) You mean—
KEN	It will be her first time.
KEN LESTER	You mean you two haven't... had a bit of *How's-your-Father*, before now?
KEN	She's... shy. I haven't even seen her in a bathing suit, for crissakes.
KEN LESTER	Bloody hell, mate. It'll 'ave been a while since you were with a first-timer.
KEN	Back then, neither party knew what the hell they were doing. Now I need to be the expert!
KEN LESTER	So... no experience at all?
KEN	I take her on my bike just so she'll wrap her arms around me. Trust me, mate, Vi has no experience in the bedroom. She's made that *very* clear.

KEN LESTER	Make sure you take a bottle of whiskey when you leave. You know… to help prime the pumps, sort of speak.
KEN	For her, or for me?
KEN LESTER	Both!
KEN	Good idea!
(TRANSITION.)	
LETTIE	This is why I kept telling you to go out with lads when you were younger. Get all the quirks out before you snag your life-long bloke. (*Touching up* VIOLET's *make-up*.)
VIOLET	Were you with… you know… that way… with *all* your lads before Tom?
LETTIE	It were my way of weeding out the losers, wasn't it? Except Percy – he were a keeper… until he wasn't.
VIOLET	You didn't want to save yourself… for your husband?
LETTIE	Nobody does that! I wanted to make sure that whoever I was going to cook, clean and raise children for, for the rest of me days, could satisfy me in… you know… make sure we were compatible.
VIOLET	And are you?
LETTIE	(*Rubbing her large belly.*) Let's just say, Tom and I *were* by the time we married. (*Chuckles.*) I just needed to train him a bit.
VIOLET	Train *him*? Bloody hell, Lettie, I have no idea what to do? What to train? Where… I've only see me brothers fully when they were bairns. Once they turned six, they kept themselves… to themselves.
LETTIE	It's cute, you know, their pee-pees, when they're bairns. But, as grown men it's… well, it's ugly. Like a big blob of dangling flesh suddenly rising…vigorously, like a … like a phoenix. Just don't look, Luv. Look anywhere… but there!

VIOLET	I need a drink!
LETTIE	Ken will have been around the block. He'll guide you.
VIOLET	How do you *know* that?
LETTIE	He were a well-travelled, handsome soldier. Trust me, he'll know what to do.
(TRANSITION.)	
KEN	Okay, Best Man, words of advice? (*Attaches* KEN's *boutonniere.*)
KEN LESTER	Take it slow, and stay in control.
(TRANSITION.)	
VIOLET	Okay, Maid of Honour – final words of advice?
LETTIE	(*Places veil on* VIOLET's *head.*) Close your eyes and grit your teeth. It'll be over before you know it. (*Sigh.*) It always is.
(TRANSITION.)	

JUNE 1951

KEN'S OLD BEDROOM IN HIS FAMILY'S HOME IN STOCKTON

(KEN *in an undershirt and trousers, stands next to his bed and* VIOLET *sits on the bed in her nightgown.*)

KEN	(*Frustrated.*) Come on, Vi, this is not right.
VIOLET	(*Upset.*) I can't, Ken.
KEN	But why? We've been married almost four months... and we haven't... you know... *consummated* our marriage yet, for heaven sakes.
VIOLET	What does that mean?
KEN	Made love! We're not even legally married... until we do.
VIOLET	I'm scared.
KEN	Of what? I'm not going to do anything that will hurt you, Luv. In fact, I think you'll enjoy—
VIOLET	It's being here.
KEN	In this room?
VIOLET	In this house! Your Mam and Dad in the room next to ours, Barry and Ted on the other side – these walls, they're paper thin—
KEN	They won't care. It's expected of a newly wedded couple.
VIOLET	I heard your Barry the other night say '*I think they might be doing it.*'
KEN	See? They're expecting it.
VIOLET	I can't! I just can't.
KEN	They're not in their rooms now. They're downstairs finishing their tea.
VIOLET	They'll soon be up to have a listen.

KEN	(*Frustrated.*) Vi, it's your… duty… as a wife.
VIOLET	(*Yells.*) I don't know what I am supposed to do.
KEN	(*Yells.*) You don't need to know. I—
VIOLET	(*Yells.*) Don't hit me!
KEN	(*Yells.*) Hit you? I would never… you think I would hit you? Crikey! Give me strength.
VIOLET	(*Yells.*) Well, you're yelling at me.
KEN	I'm yelling… (*Stops. Sympathetic.*) I would never hit you, Vi – never! I need you to know that. I was raised better than that. (*Takes her hands in his.*) I'm sorry I yelled. It's just that I'm… I'm…
VIOLET	I'm too old to start… me body… down there, well… it won't be able to handle your… you know… I needed to have been… *broken* earlier.
KEN	(*Laughs.*) Where did you hear that load of rubbish?
VIOLET	(*Starts to cry.*) Don't laugh at me
KEN	I'm not laughing at you, Luv. I'm laughing at the daft notion that you think—
VIOLET	See, you think I'm daft.
KEN	I don't mean *you're* daft. What you've been *told* is daft. Did your Mam not tell you about… stuff?
VIOLET	Not a dickey-bird. I think me-Mam figured I would never… Oh, I don't know. Did your dad tell you about… stuff?
KEN	When I was 14 and left school, he shoved a sheath in my hand and said, *Lad, mind your P's and Q's and then put a sock in it, and on it, or lose your freedom.* And that was that. The rest… well, I found out by trial and error. (*Chuckles.*)

VIOLET	I don't know the ways of the world, what to believe, what *not* to believe. I don't know what a wife is *supposed* to do – in the bedroom. I only know how to cook and clean. I tried to tell you, before we married. I knew you would need a wife who was… experienced. I knew!
KEN	You're wrong, Vi. I don't need a housekeeper. I need a wife, a *partner* who can trust me and who I can trust in return.
VIOLET	I *do* trust you.
KEN	(*Tender.*) Making love will bring us closer, Luv. (*Wipes the tears from her cheek.*) Grow our love. That's what making love means.
VIOLET	But I do love you, so much already.
KEN	It's more intimate – makes us… one.
VIOLET	See how smart you are?
KEN	I think I read that in a book from the library. (*Chuckles.*)
VIOLET	You know things I didn't even know, that I didn't know. (*Chuckles.*)
KEN	We all find out in our own good time, Vi. (*Pause.*) So, do you want to… deepen our love? I know I do.
VIOLET	I think I do, but… I… it doesn't feel intimate when I can hear your brothers sniggering in the next room.
KEN	Wait here! (*Storms out of the room. EXIT. Off.*) Alright everyone – out! (*Murmur.*) You heard me. Clear off! (*Murmur.*) Everyone out of the house, now! Shift yourself. Now! (*Murmur.*) I don't care where you go I just need you out of here for a couple of hours. (*Murmur.*) Don't faff about, Barry! Get yourself off to the pictures. Here, Ted, take this. Treat yourself to an ice-lolly. (*Door slams. ENTER.*) Right, that's taken care of. Now where were we?
VIOLET	What did you just do?

KEN	I've sent them to the pictures.
VIOLET	All of them?
KEN	It's just the two of us now, Luv.
VIOLET	Why?
KEN	(*Anxious.*) So we can… Violet, I want to love you with every part of my being. Please!
VIOLET	I told you, I don't know how!
KEN	We'll take it slow.
VIOLET	(*Takes a big breath.*) Okay. (*She shuts her eyes tight and grits her teeth.*) Go ahead.
KEN	What are you doing?
VIOLET	(*With clenched teeth.*) Closing my eyes and gritting my teeth.
KEN	(*Chuckles.*) Nay, lass, you're not having a bullet removed. (*Tender.*) I'm just going to kiss you… here. (*Pecks her on the forehead.*) Was that so bad?
VIOLET	(*Ungrits her teeth.*) No.
KEN	Now I'm going to kiss you… here. (*Pecks her on her cheek.*) Still alright?
VIOLET	(*Opens her eyes.*) Yes.
KEN	Now I want to kiss you… on your lips.
VIOLET	We've done that before. (*Smiles.*)
KEN	And it was lovely. (*Kisses her on the lips.*)
VIOLET	I do like that.
KEN	Now I'm going to lay you down on the bed.
VIOLET	(*Big breath.*) Okay.

KEN	Ever so gently. (*Lays her slowly on the bed.*) Now, I'm going to slide your nightie off—
VIOLET	(*Tenses up.*) Ummm
KEN	Off your shoulder... like this. And I'm going to kiss your soft skin. (*Kisses her shoulder.*) Your neck. (*Kisses her neck.*)
VIOLET	That feels nice.
KEN	Keep looking into my eyes, Luv.
VIOLET	I will.
KEN	(*Takes off his shirt and lowers himself onto* VIOLET.) My beautiful Violet.

(TRANSITION.)

CHRISTMAS DAY 1951

THE TURK'S HEAD PUB IN STOCKTON

SFX – SOFT SOUNDS OF CHRISTMAS MUSIC AND A MURMUR OF CHATTER IN A CROWDED PUB IN THE BACKGROUND.

(KEN LESTER *and* LETTIE *sit in the snug.*)

LETTIE	Wonder what the news is?
KEN LESTER	Hope they'll be here soon. Sheila's only given me an hour.
LETTIE	How's Christmas going, then? (*Lights a cigarette.*)
KEN LESTER	Our Christine's too young to know about Father Christmas, but Sheila's been baking all month, so lots of treats. They've been sitting in the pantry with the word *temptation* inscribed on every crumb. She won't let me sample – not even one. (*Chuckles.*) And you?
LETTIE	Geoffrey's still a baby – hasn't got a clue – thank goodness. No visit from Father Christmas this year. But we have a goose for tea. It's in the oven now, so I can't dawdle. Where are they?
VIOLET	(ENTER. *Joins them in the snug.*) Happy Christmas, Lettie, Luv. (*Gives a big hug*.)
LETTIE	Happy Christmas, Vi.
VIOLET	Where's Tom?
LETTIE	He took our Geoffrey for a quick visit to his sister Linda's in Middlesborough.
VIOLET	You didn't want to go?
LETTIE	Are you bloody kidding me? She thinks I'm as common as muck. She thinks her Tom married beneath himself! He's only a postman! And he keeps his gob shut when she starts up. It just leads to a bunch of argy-bargy – I get enough of that with me own Mam.

VIOLET	(*Laughing. To* KEN LESTER.) Happy Christmas, Ken. (*They hug.*)
KEN LESTER	Happy Christmas, Luv.
VIOLET	Where's Sheila?
KEN LESTER	Getting the Christmas dinner ready, isn't she? Her parents are coming over. She's only given me an hour to wet me whistle – need to get back to peel the spuds.
VIOLET	My Ken could help you there. (*Chuckles.*)
LETTIE	She's got a right leash on you, Ken Lester.
KEN	(ENTER. *Arrives at snug with drinks on a tray.*) Here you go, then. (*Divvy's out drinks.*) And for you, Luv. (*Puts a glass of orange juice in front of* VI.)
LETTIE	Not drinking, Vi?
VIOLET	Not today.
LETTIE	But it's Christmas!
VIOLET	(*Big smile.*) Yeah, but... I'm having a baby, aren't I?
LETTIE	You what?
KEN LESTER	(*To* KEN.) Congratulations old man! Welcome to the club – I think.
LETTIE	(*Hugs* VIOLET.) Oh Vi, I'm so chuffed for you. When are you due?
VIOLET	August. (*Lights up a cigarette.*)
KEN	This will be our last Christmas amongst the rubble and ash.
KEN LESTER	Who you calling rubble and ash? (*Chuckles.*)
LETTIE	Take that back, Ken Clarke! I get enough of that from Linda.
KEN	Keep your hair on! (*Laughing.*) I mean Stockton!
LETTIE	Where are you off to, then?

KEN	Australia–
LETTIE	Ya-never!
KEN LESTER	Taking advantage of that 10-Pound-Pom program their offering?
LETTIE	(*To* VIOLET.) That's on the other side of the world!
VIOLET	Canada first.
KEN	I've promised Vi that if things don't work out, we'll return to England. That Aussie immigration ploy requires a two-year commitment to stay. And if we want to leave sooner, the passage will cost us close to a year's wage.
KEN LESTER	I thought it sounded too good. Who knows what they'll take advantage of once you're there.
VIOLET	So, we'll give Canada a go first.
LETTIE	Still far away!
KEN LESTER	Lots of good paying jobs going for ex-soldiers of the British Army in the colonies. You do right!
KEN	Thanks, mate!
KEN LESTER	It'll take time for Britain to recover from the bloody war. *Still* rationing stuff!
LETTIE	Canada and Australia were in the war too.
KEN	But their cities didn't get pummeled like ours.
LETTIE	When are you off?
KEN	I'm heading over in March.
KEN LESTER	Uhhh, I'm totally jealous.
LETTIE	What about Vi? (*To* VI.) You can't be travelling the world in your condition.

KEN	Vi will be staying with her Mam and Dad's until the baby's born.
KEN LESTER	You heading over on your *own*? Our Sheila would never allow that.
KEN	This is how Vi wants to do it, don't you, Luv?
VIOLET	Yes. I want to stay… to have the baby here… with me-Mam.
KEN	I've already started the process for us to immigrate to Canada. And once I'm there I'll apply for further immigration to Australia.
KEN LESTER	That won't be a problem since they're part of the Commonwealth.
KEN	Exactly. Once Vi arrives in Canada—
LETTIE	With a baby!
KEN	With our baby, we'll stay there for a couple of years – and then save for the travel across Canada, and then the trans-pacific crossing—
LETTIE	(*To* VIOLET.) You're actually going to get out of this hell-hole and see the world. Good on you, Luv. Wait 'til I tell our Tom. He'll be right pissed that he missed this!
KEN	Maybe keep it to yourselves… for now.
LETTIE	Absolutely. (VIOLET *rolls her eyes*.) But I can tell Tom, right?
VIOLET	Will he want to emigrate too? Talk to him about it, Lettie.
LETTIE	Oh, I could see his sister's face, if we did. (*Laugh*.) It would be worth emigrating just for that.
VIOLET	Seriously. Ask Tom. And Ken, ask Sheila.
KEN	Sure, the more the merrier. We could start our own commune. (*Chuckles*.)

KEN LESTER	Like gypsies! Ooo, that would put our Sheila right off. She can't stand neighbours who keep to themselves, let alone live near friends.
LETTIE	(*To* VIOLET.) I can't believe you actually want to do this. You really want to go?
KEN	Passports arrived last week.
VIOLET	(*Not convincing.*) As Ken says, it's a good start for us.
LETTIE	Nobody's twisting your arm or anything, are they?
KEN	What are you saying, Lettie?
VIOLET	We need a place of our own to live. We can't keep living with Ken's family.
KEN LESTER	I'm surprised you lasted this long in that wee house.
KEN	I can't believe I moved back in! But with our Vern in Sheffield for university, there was room. I mean, our Barry was upset, thinking he would finally get a room of his own, but he'll soon be off to join the Merchant Marines.
LETTIE	Then he still won't get a room of his own. Poor sod! (*Laughs.*)
KEN	Staying with my family was the only way to save up.
VIOLET	And there will be more career opportunities for Ken, so we'll be able to buy a house of our own.
KEN	Me-Mam has right enjoyed having our Vi living with her— a bit of female company in a house full of lads. But it will be different when a baby comes along.
KEN LESTER	In more ways than you think, mate!
VIOLET	Ken will send over a ticket for me and the baby to cross the Atlantic by next Christmas. He's got it all worked out.
LETTIE	You – Violet Macdonald are—
KEN	Violet *Clarke*.

LETTIE	Oh, right. (*Choking up.*) I'll miss you something awful!
VIOLET	(*Choking up.*) Me too!
LETTIE	(*Takes* VIOLET's *hand.*) Maybe you have some of that Robert the Bruce in you after all! I don't think I would be brave enough to travel the ocean in a boat… on me own… with a wee baby.
KEN	Ships are the safest way to travel.
LETTIE	Tell that to the passengers of the Titanic.
VIOLET	(*Stands up.*) Excuse me! (*Starts to cry.*) I need to use the loo. (EXITS.)
LETTIE	(*Shouting after her.*) You alright, Luv? (*To* KEN.) I don't think she's alright with all this, Ken.
KEN	She knows it's our best chance to buy a home and raise a family in a war-free country. Goodness knows when Britain will be back at it – fighting the bloody good fight.
LETTIE	True enough! Maybe it's just morning sickness. It can be brutal. You blokes haven't got a clue what you put us women through.
KEN LESTER	I am totally jealous of you, mate, but definitely pleased for you both.
LETTIE	You have a job lined up over there?
KEN	No, but I hope to be taken on as a police officer – either in Canada or Australia. I'm already trained.
KEN LESTER	They'll take you, no prob – as long as they don't ask to read your army records. (*Chuckles.*)
LETTIE	Coppers don't make much.
KEN	They do once you start to move up the ranks!
LETTIE	Like you did in the army?
KEN LESTER	Oh, she got you there. (*Chuckles.*)

KEN	We could use a little support here, Lettie.
LETTIE	You can buy a council house here, you know. Tom and I just put our names in last month. Priority is given to ex-servicemen who are married *with* children.
KEN	No offense, Lettie, but I don't want to rely on any handouts.
LETTIE	Getting a bit above yourself, aren't you, Guv?
KEN	Truth is, I've had enough of this place. It's too predictable - no job promotion – unless you're in the right circles.
KEN LESTER	And shipyards are closing – not to mention manufacturing's at a standstill.
KEN	Exactly, mate! To make a better life for ourselves we'd have to move out of Yorkshire anyway. Go south. Why not go the whole hog?
KEN LESTER	The colonies are where the opportunities lie now.
LETTIE	You could work on cars – you do that – it's a good skill. Everyone's starting to buy them now and need blokes to keep them in good nick.
KEN	I want more than—
KEN LESTER	Have you told them at Hills yet?
KEN	They don't need to know anything until I'm ready to go. They'll soon find someone else. Anyone with a license can drive their trucks of sawdust to the incinerators.
KEN LESTER	Yes, but you also fixed their trucks when they broke down.
KEN	Didn't pay me extra for that, though, did they? (*To* LETTIE.) But for now, mum's-the-word.
LETTIE	(*Zips her lips. Whispers.*) Of course!
KEN LESTER	Where in Canada? It looks huge on the map, like Russia.
KEN	I dock in Montreal. So we'll start there.

LETTIE	Has Vi told her Mam and Dad yet?
KEN	We will, after Christmas. They're enjoying the news of the baby just now.
LETTIE	Her Mam will be heartbroken, as will her Aunty Gladdy and Maureen. They're very close.
KEN	It *will* be hard at first, we know, but they can come and visit. Our door will always be open… and to you.
KEN LESTER	What about your family? Have you told them?
KEN	Not yet. Me-Mam will be sad to see us go. Well, mostly Vi, and of course the baby. But she still has our Ted to keep her busy. (*Chuckles.*)
LETTIE	(*Finishes her drink in one gulp and stands.*) I think I'll check on Vi. See how she *really* feels about all this. (EXITS.)
KEN	(*Shouts after her.*) She's fine about it. Really!
KEN LESTER	You do right, leaving this place.
KEN	I've had a taste of the world, mate. I just feel like I'll smother and wither away if I stay.
KEN LESTER	I wish our Sheila was more adventurous.
KEN	Tell me something, would you have married Sheila, you know… if you knew her better and hadn't… you know… put her in the family way?
KEN LESTER	I think so. (*Pause.*) I hope so. But Vi… she really alright with it all?
KEN	Naturally, she's apprehensive. But, she said if it's what I want, she would support me. It seems to be more important for her to stay and have the baby here – with her Mam.
KEN LESTER	Sheila wanted her Mam too. Didn't want me anywhere near her – for months. Well, it looks like she's over her hesitancy in the bedroom now. Vi, I mean, not Sheila. (*Chuckles.*)

KEN	I was worried in the beginning, if I'm honest. It took a few goes, but I think it's safe to say, we won't be having any issues in *that* area again. Everything now works as it should.
KEN LESTER	(*Raises his glass.*) Cheers to that! And to your new life abroad!
KEN	(*Raises his glass.*) Thanks, mate. Cheers!
(TRANSITION.)	

MARCH – DECEMBER, 1952

(*In a spotlight,* KEN *speaks as he writes his letters to* VIOLET. *In a separate more muted spotlight, simultaneous action takes place in silence, except for SFX.*)

KEN	ACTION
My dearest Violet, My first letter to you since arriving in Canada. The crossing on the Empress of France was a bit rough around the Sea of Labrador but they said that was to be expected this time of year. It should be calmer when you set off later in the year. I landed in Montreal but found everyone spoke mostly French. One of my fellow passengers said I would have a better chance of a job further west in the city of Toronto. I'm heading there in a couple of days. (*New letter.*) I finally made it to Toronto. It's very much like London. Lots of cars, people and buses. Tall buildings. Everything you need and want all on your doorstep. And everyone speaks English! Lots of Brits here, too. (*New letter.*) I found a job. Not with the police, as I had hoped. I underwent an eye exam during my application and apparently, I need glasses! And they don't hire blokes who require glasses.	VIOLET *sits and reads* KEN's *letter.* VIOLET *sits and writes a letter to* KEN VIOLET *sits and reads* KEN's *letter.* VIOLET *walks towards a table, visible in her final stages of pregnancy and folds laundry. At one point she doubles over with a contraction.* VIOLET *in a night gown is now lying on a bed going through labour.* AGNES *is with her holding her hand.* SFX - CRY OF A BABY.

Even after me spouting all my credentials of being in the British Military Police and my travels to foreign lands, they said they had plenty of similar qualified applicants but who had better eyesight. The job I did get is in a warehouse. A company called Massey-Harris. They build tractors for farms, so I was well-in there.

Hopefully recruiting restrictions for police officers in Australia will be more in my favour.

(*New letter.*) A baby girl! Hope all went well and that your Mam gave you all the support you needed. I found us a place to live – just temporary, mind you – until we buy a house of our own. I need to be employed for at least six months to secure a mortgage with the bank. The rent is manageable and it's near my job and a beautiful park called High Park. The family who owns the house, Joan and Pat, emigrated from Ireland a few years ago and are quite settled. They live on the main level and we will be renting the 2nd and 3rd floor. Pat renovated it himself. It truly is a work of exceptional craftsmanship. The best news though, is they have a wee baby girl just like us. Only a few months older. | AGNES *wraps baby in a blanket and hands to an exhausted but joyful* VIOLET.

VIOLET *sits happily in a rocking chair feeding her baby with a bottle. She puts baby in a cot nearby.*

VIOLET *in a dress, excitedly writes a letter to* KEN *about their new baby.*

VIOLET *wearing a hat, stands at the altar of a church holding the baby in a blanket. A* VICAR *stands opposite her.*

VIOLET *hands the baby over to* VICAR *for a blessing ritual. She takes out a hanky to wipe a tear.* AGNES *joins* VIOLET *and puts her arm around her.*

VIOLET *reads* KEN's *letter.*

VIOLET *cries in* AGNES's *arms.* |

And you'll never guess, Joan had a whip around with all her mum friends in the neighbourhood and they have set you up with a cot, pram, high chair and few bits and bobs for the kitchen. I'll sort out some furnishings before you arrive. You might not recognize me when you see me next, I wear glasses now. Still getting use to wearing them – especially with the safety goggles, which I'm required to wear at work. The good news is that my work paid for them. Part of the benefits package. I'm doing well with the job. I think they may promote me soon. It will give us more money to save for Australia.

(*New letter.*) I purchased your ticket for the Queen Mary. I will send it by special delivery so you receive it well in advance of your departure from Southampton. It's a big ship and relatively new, so you will feel quite safe. With your ticket will be your immigration papers. Just sign where I have marked and bring them with you. Ken can help you if you need it. I wrote to Ken asking him to take you to the Passport Office in Middlesborough to have Rose added to your passport. Still getting use to having a baby girl. I can't wait to meet her. You arrive in New York on Christmas Day.

(*New letter.*) The autumn here is beautiful.

VIOLET *wears a winter coat, gloves and scarf on her head, holds baby wrapped in a blanket. A large worn suitcase and baby bag are at her feet. She is saying her good-bye's to* AGNES *and* ERNIE *with lots of tears and hugs.*

SFX – A SHIP'S HORN.

She finally turns, picks up her suitcase. AGNES *helps her put the baby bag on her shoulder, and walks up the gangplank, both crying.* AGNES *returns to* ERNIE *who consoles her as they wave their final good-byes.*

VIOLET *nervously sits on a chair in her cabin wearing a sweater over her dress, rocking her baby. The ship's* PURSER *approaches to encourage her to come with him. She stays put. He gives up.*

SFX – SHIP'S HORN BLOWS

VIOLET *with baby in her arms, is swaying and bracing herself from stormy seas, scared.*

The colours of the trees are brilliant, like nothing I've seen before. They keep the streets so clean and flower baskets are hung over almost every shop entrance. What a difference to the soot and grime of Stockton high street.

(*New letter*.) Happy birthday, Luv. It won't be long now. It's been almost eight months since I left. I miss you so much. How is life with baby Rose? Still wrapping my head around being a father! Me-Mam said you had been around and that she's a little flower. And pass on my congratulations to Tom and Lettie. She'll have her hands full with Geoffrey and baby being so close in age. I know you will miss them very much. I'll be waiting for you once you go through immigration. Look for the bloke with the black rimmed specs. (*Chuckles*.) See you and baby Rose soon. All my love, Daddy-Ken. (*EXITS*.)

VIOLET *is picking at a dinner plate, wiping tears from her cheek. Checks on her baby and returns to the dinner only to push it away.*

SFX – SHIP'S HORN BLOWS

The PURSER *enters to let* VIOLET *know they are close to port.* VIOLET *excitedly packs baby items in the baby bag and few personal items in her suitcase and closes it. She puts her coat, gloves and scarf on, bundles her baby up in a big blanket and hurriedly exits with great joy.*

SFX – SOUND OF SEAGULLS AND WIND

VIOLET, *for the 1st time since boarding the ship, with the wind blowing and baby wrapped in a blanket, is on the deck taking in the sea air and looking with great anticipation of docking and seeing* KEN *once again. EXITS.*

Blooming Violet

December 25, 1952

TERMINAL OF THE NEW YORK CITY PIER

SFX – CROWDS IN BACKGROUND

KEN (*Waving madly.*) Vi! Over here! Vi!

VIOLET (ENTERS.) Ken! Ken!

KEN (*Takes suitcase.*) Let me take that, Luv.

VIOLET Just hold me! Please! Hold me and never let me go.

KEN (*Drops case. Hugs her.*) Oh Vi, Luv – I missed you so much.

VIOLET I missed you too.

KEN (*Looks her in the eyes.*) I'm so proud of you. You did it! You made it!

VIOLET (*Retreats back. Firm.*) I will tell you summat for nowt, Ken Clarke, I will never travel on a boat, big or small, ever again in my life. Do you hear me?

KEN Just one more, Luv – to Australia.

VIOLET No! Not one!

KEN But the plan—

VIOLET No! I'm done travelling.

KEN Was it a rough crossing?

VIOLET Never again!

KEN Oh, Vi. I'm sorry it was scary for you—

VIOLET *And* for Rose!

KEN Rose! Here she is – our little Rose petal. Let me have a look.

VIOLET (*Softening.*) She was a real trooper, Ken. Unlike me, she slept. I think the rumble of the engines helped. But not me!

KEN	I should have paid for a cabin higher up in the ship, away from the engines – maybe with a porthole, to look out of. Quite a bit more money but—
VIOLET	It wouldn't have made a bit of difference. But, our Rose… do you want to hold her?
KEN	Ahhh, maybe not right now.
VIOLET	She's your daughter!
KEN	I know, I know… I just… I would be more comfortable sitting down. You know, so I don't drop her.
VIOLET	(*Laughs.*) Don't be daft, you won't drop her.
KEN	I've never held a wee baby before.
VIOLET	Take her! (*She places* ROSE *in* KEN's *arms.*) Mind her head. Keep her head firm in the crook of your arm.
KEN	(*Nervous. Awkward.*) I'm not sure…
VIOLET	(*Fussing.*) You'll soon get the hang of it. Wait 'til you have to change her nappy. (*Laughs. Opens blanket so he can see* ROSE's *face.*) There you go!
KEN	(*Looking adoringly at* ROSE *in his arms.*) Oh Vi, Luv – she's beautiful. Look at her!
VIOLET	I do, all day long. (*Chuckles.*)
KEN	(*Can't take his eyes off* ROSE.) Look what we did – what we made together.
VIOLET	You did the *easy* part.
KEN	Did everything go alright? You know, with having her? You didn't say much in your letters. (*To* ROSE.) Hello, little one.
VIOLET	Yes – well as much as can be expected, apparently. No complications. And I'm almost healed now, so that's good.
KEN	You'll be back in the saddle in no time then. (*Chuckles.*) (*To* ROSE.) I'm your Da-da.

VIOLET	Not for a while, Mr. Clarke! (*Chuckles.*) By the way, I like your new specs. They look good on you.
KEN	(*Awkwardly with* ROSE *in his arms, shifts his glasses up his nose as they are a little loose.*) I didn't realize I needed specs until I started wearing them. Everything's crystal clear now.
VIOLET	They make you look... more intelligent. (*They both chuckle.*)
KEN	You managed customs alright, then? I've been here a few hours waiting – you know, just in case. (*To* ROSE, *tickles her under the chin.*) Cootchie-cootchie-coo!
VIOLET	(*Fusses over* ROSE.) Keep the blanket wrapped around her. Yes, everything was in order, like you sent. No problems. Just need to get to Canada now. By land!
KEN	I have bus tickets for us. We leave in a few hours. We can grab a cab to the Station. (*Gives* ROSE *back to* VIOLET.)
VIOLET	Can we get a bite to eat first, I'm starving!
KEN	Didn't they feed you well on the ship? I know you were in third class, but the meals were supposed to be— (*Picks up suitcase.*)
VIOLET	I'm sure they were. I just had tea an' toast. Me stomach was churning the whole time and I didn't want to be sick.
KEN	Not much open today, being Christmas Day, an' all. But I did notice a cafe about five minutes away.
VIOLET	That'll do. It's cold out here. (*Shivers.*) I'm gasping for a cup of tea. And I need to warm up a bottle for our Rose.
KEN	Hmmm... you'll find the tea will fall short of what you're used to. They're big on coffee here.
VIOLET	At this point, I don't care. (*They start walking.*) I'm glad you were alright with us having our Rose christened at home. Me-Mam really wanted her... well, in case summat happened on the crossing.

KEN (*Chuckles.*) I'm not much of a churchgoer, so, if it was important to you, Luv...

VIOLET For me-Mam, it was. I should let you know that I gave our Rose a middle name.

KEN You did? They're reserved for the aristocracy. (*Chuckles.*) We're not there... yet.

VIOLET It's becoming quite popular with us plebs now. (*Chuckles.*) Lettie called her baby girl, Sandra *Rebecca* – Rebecca after Tom's mom. Drove her sister-in-law, Linda, crazy. (*Laughs.*)

KEN What's *our Lady's* middle name then?

VIOLET It was going to be Gladys, you know, after me Auntie, but then I changed me mind. I named her Rose Maureen.

KEN After your sister?

VIOLET Rose Maureen Clarke. Yes, after our Maureen.

KEN She would like that.

VIOLET Well, our Maureen had to forgo her 21st birthday celebration, you see – when Rose was born – with it being just a couple of weeks later. Our Rose and I had taken over the front room, so there were no space. I knew she were disappointed, even though she didn't say. So when I told her that she would be Rose's namesake – middle name, anyway – she were over the moon.

KEN I can't wait for you to see Toronto. You'll love it. I just know it. And the family we share the house with – they're very excited to meet you.

VIOLET I thought for sure you would've been able to buy a house of our own by now. What with all we had saved before you left, your job at the tractor place... and all that talk about the land of opportunity and—

KEN (*Sheepish.*) I ya, didn't have enough down payment.

VIOLET	(*Interrogative*.) Hold on! You wrote that your job paid well. You've been grafting at this Massey what's-it's-name place since—
KEN	(*Sheepish*.) I needed to buy some transportation, you know, to get to and from work.
VIOLET	(*Stops in her tracks*.) You wrote that our flat was close to your work. Besides, they have buses – you said so in your letters.
KEN	Well yes, but, for extra money, I work the odd night-shift and the buses don't run late.
VIOLET	(*Starts to walk again*.) I guess we do need a car, now that we're a family – especially if winters in Canada are *this* snowy and cold – and, of course, for outings and such.
KEN	Oh!
VIOLET	What?
KEN	(*Hesitant*.) I don't think I thought this through?
VIOLET	(*Stops*.) What do you mean?
KEN	(*Stops*.) I bought a bike.
VIOLET	(*Taken back*.) A motorbike?
KEN	Got a good deal.
VIOLET	You bought a motorbike with our down payment money?
KEN	It was on its last legs, but I—
VIOLET	(*Angry*.) Kenneth Clarke! You selfish man! Do you know what I have been through?
KEN	I know you—
VIOLET	(*Angry*.) What I have given up?
KEN	Yes, of course, but—

VIOLET	(*Tearing up.*) Saying good-bye to my family, Me-Mam, Me-Dad, our Maureen, Malcolm, Timmy, Dennis... Aunty Gladdy—
KEN	We knew it would be hard—
VIOLET	(*Stifled shout.*) Your family...
KEN	They understand—
VIOLET	(*Stifled shout.*) Our friends?
KEN	Lettie will be busy with—
VIOLET	(*Shouts.*) Lettie will *still* be crying!
KEN	(*Looking around.*) Keep your voice down—
VIOLET	(*Tone changes to firm.*) Don't you tell *me* what to do. (*Voice starts to crack.*) I left my best friend – with her new baby girl, who would have grown up to be best friends with our Rose—
KEN	Vi, Luv, it's going to be—
VIOLET	Leaving all what is comfortable, all that I know, to come to a... a foreign land!
KEN	It's not too foreign—
VIOLET	Trusting – yes *trusting*, all your talk about a better life!
KEN	It will be. You just need to—
VIOLET	(*Shouts.*) My piano!!!!
KEN	I'm sorry, I—
VIOLET	(*Pulling herself together. Firm.*) You will sell that bike as soon as we arrive in Toronto, sir. You can purchase a pushbike to use when the buses don't run. And we'll start to save as much as we can until we buy a house to call our own. Do you hear me?
KEN	(*Smiles.*) Listen to you?

VIOLET	(*Firm.*) No! You listen to me! Do you hear me?
KEN	(*Salutes.*) Loud and clear, Sarge. (*Ernest.*) Listen, Vi, Luv, I… I… I'm so sorry. I know this was hard… to leave… and I promise you, it will be worth it. I… I will make this right. I will.
VIOLET	(*Firm.*) No, Ken, *we* will make it right! We're a family now. There is no *just Ken* or *just Vi*. We have wee Rose Maureen to think about now. It's all what's best for *her*… for *us*, as a family, from now on.
KEN	I'll buy you a new piano, as soon as—
VIOLET	No, Ken! Spending our hard-earned money on a piano *now* is *not* what's best for our Rose.
KEN	(*Impressed.*) Wow! Where did my *shrinking* Violet go?
VIOLET	Oh, she's *long* gone. You know, I always thought I needed a man, a husband, to get me through life… but… me Aunty Gladdy were right… what I really needed was for me… *me*… to believe in meself – trust me *own* decisions.
KEN	Mrs. Clarke, you *have* come into your own!
VIOLET	Not of my choosing, mind, but… yes, I suppose I have. (*Realization.*) All those months – without you, becoming a mother – without you, leaving all who I knew, travelling half way around the world… without you… heck, if I can do all *that*, I guess… no, I *know*… I can look after meself… and our Rose. (*Proud.*) And about time, too!
KEN	(*Bemused.*) You're not writing me off *yet*, are you?
VIOLET	(*Softens.*) Not yet. But I'm not who you left behind in England, Ken.
KEN	No, you are *not*. But, I like this new you! I like it a lot.

VIOLET (*Starts walking again.*) Come on our Rose Maureen, let's get your Mam fueled up with a nice cuppa. She's got her work cut out for her. (*To* KEN.) Well, stop faffing about there, daddy, shift yourself!

KEN I'm coming! (*Picks up suitcase and joins her.*) I'm so happy you're finally here, Vi, Luv. (*Puts his arm around her.*)

VIOLET And not a moment too soon, I'd say. (*Smiles.*) Not a moment too soon. Happy Christmas, Ken. (*Snuggles into* KEN *as they walk away together. Both* EXIT.)

THE END

Violet Macdonald
21st Birthday - 1944

Sergeant Macdonald
W.A.C. - 1948

Vi & Ken
Pub in Stockton-on-Tees -1950

www.ingramcontent.com/pod-product-compliance
Lightning Source LLC
Chambersburg PA
CBHW080610170426
43209CB00007B/1392